20 PROGRAMS
FOR THE
ZX SPECTRUM & 16K ZX81

ALSO BY THE SAME AUTHOR

BP86: An Introduction to BASIC Programming Techniques

20 PROGRAMS
FOR THE
ZX SPECTRUM & 16K ZX81

by
S. DALY, M.B.C.S.

**BERNARD BABANI (publishing) LTD
THE GRAMPIANS
SHEPHERDS BUSH ROAD
LONDON W6 7NF
ENGLAND**

PLEASE NOTE

Although every care has been taken with the production of this book to ensure that any projects, designs, modifications and/or programs etc. contained herein, operate in a correct and safe manner and also that any components specified are normally available in Great Britain, the Publishers do not accept responsibility in any way for the failure, including fault in design, of any project, design, modification or program to work correctly or to cause damage to any other equipment that it may be connected to or used in conjunction with, or in respect of any other damage or injury that may be so caused, nor do the Publishers accept responsibility in any way for the failure to obtain specified components.

Notice is also given that if equipment that is still under warranty is modified in any way or used or connected with home-built equipment then that warranty may be void.

© 1983 BERNARD BABANI (publishing) LTD

First Published — October 1983

British Cataloguing in Publication Data
Daly, S.
  20 programs for the ZX Spectrum
  & 16K ZX81. —(BP128)
  1. Sinclair ZX Spectrum (Computer) — Programming
  2. Sinclair ZX81 (Computer) — Programming
  I. Title
  001.64'2   QA76.8.S625

  ISBN 0 85934 103 8

Printed and bound in Great Britain by Cox & Wyman Ltd, Reading

FOREWORD

In preparing a collection of programs for the home computer enthusiast I thought it wise to adopt certain guidelines. The first was to choose a standard computer BASIC so I decided upon the popular Sinclair BASIC as used on *Spectrum* and the *ZX81*. However, the programs should be readily loaded onto other systems. This precluded the use of PEEK/POKE, machine code routines and the various graphics symbols which are peculiar to particular machines.

I was also determined to write the programs as simply as I could and to avoid special statements that are not widely available. Where special Sinclair features had to be used (as in string handling) notes have been added to show other users the way to adapt the programs to run on their system.

Being interested myself in loading published programs it has often occurred to me how useful flow charts are to the understanding of programs. These are especially helpful when adapting a program to run on another system. They also help when improving or modifying a program. I have also found descriptions of what happens when you run a program useful. Consequently both these features are included.

Since detailed explanations on how to run the programs are given, the usual verbose text embedded in numerous PRINT statements is not. If required you can easily add them yourself. If there are insufficient gaps between the existing line numbers to say all you want you can utilise GOSUB/RETURN.

More experienced programmers may want to improve on the programs and some suggestions are given within the text. Again, the detailed explanation behind the thinking and logic given here should help them considerably. Similarly the novice programmer can gain insights into the various techniques employed in complex programming situations.

To save time you may not want to enter all the REM statements. However, before omitting any please check that they are not required by a GOTO or GOSUB statement. The wisest policy is to just enter the line number followed by REM on its own.

A major problem with publications containing program listings is accuracy. To avoid type-setting errors the programs have been loaded onto a computer, checked that they then run and have then been dumped to a printer. The actual print-out was used to prepare the plates used in printing. When proof copies were available the programs were punched up from the proofs onto a computer and again checked.

As I mentioned in my previous book, "An Introduction to BASIC Programming Techniques: BP86" also published by Babani Books, another type of error can creep in to the most carefully prepared program. This can occur when you have a large number of logic paths and any error may only show up infrequently. To counter this I have used versions of the programs that I have had for some time and I have resisted the temptation to change anything even when a more elegant approach suggested itself. In addition a couple of friends have loaded the programs onto their computers and checked them. If in spite of all this some bugs remain the detailed program description and flow charts show the logic I have employed so the enthusiast should be able to correct matters himself.

Finally I would like to thank *Chris Malsom* for loading and testing these programs on his *Spectrum*, *Bob Howells* for doing a similar job with his *VIC20*, *Chris Osborne* for loading the engineering programs on his *PET* and *Severn Software* of Lydney who enabled me to print out the programs.

S. Daly

CONTENTS

Page

Chapter 1: CONVERTING PROGRAMS WRITTEN IN ONE DIALECT TO ANOTHER 1
Sinclair BASIC 2
Cards 3
   How to Play 5
Biorhythms 10

Chapter 2: CARD GAMES 15
Shuffle 15
Brag 17
   Notes on Brag Version Used 17
   Program Description 18
Pontoon 27
   The Pontoon Flow Chart 29
   Program Notes 29

Chapter 3: MORE GAMES 35
Battleships 35
   Notes for Non-Sinclair Users 36
Solitaire 41
   Solitaire Program Notes 43
Calendar 48

Chapter 4: SORTING 54
Alpha Sort Program 54

Chapter 5: FILING SYSTEMS 60
Files 60
   Addendum 64
Italian 65

Chapter 6: ENGINEERING APPLICATIONS 71
Complex Numbers – the j Operator 71
Binary/Hexadecimal/Decimal Conversion 76
   Binary to Decimal 76
   Decimal to Binary 76

	Page
Binary to Hexadecimal	76
Hexadecimal to Binary	77
Decimal to Hexadecimal	77
Hexadecimal to Decimal	77
Running Instructions	79
Superhet	93
Chapter 7: STATISTICS	**100**
Binomal	100
Exponential (Poisson)	103
Runs-test	105
ESP	109
Odds and Ends	111
Appendix 1: Solitaire Solution	**113**
Appendix 2: Alternative Version of Complex Number Routine	**114**

Chapter 1

CONVERTING PROGRAMS WRITTEN IN ONE DIALECT TO ANOTHER

From experience this can prove difficult. The way to achieve it is to try to understand what the original program is doing (this may require access to the manual for the original BASIC). Once you know what the program does it is a relatively simple matter to re-write it in your own dialect. Hopefully the programs in this book are explained in great detail and, of course, you will not have recourse to a Sinclair manual if your computer happens to be some other marque.

I have found that it is essential to have sufficient gaps between lines of the original program. For instance consider:

```
100 INPUT A,B,C,D
110 LET S=A+B+C+D
```

Some computers cannot accommodate the input of several variables in one line so we would have to adjust the program thus:

```
100 INPUT A
102 INPUT B
104 INPUT C
106 INPUT D
110 LET S=A+B+C+D
```

If there aren't sufficient gaps between lines you may have a RENUMBER facility. In this case enter the program apart from problem lines and renumber it with 10 or 20 between line numbers.

Some systems can't handle complex logic such as:

```
20 IF A=5 AND B=7 THEN LET C=25
40 REM
```

A way around this would be

```
20 IF A=5 THEN 35
```

```
25 GOTO 40
35 IF B=7 THEN LET C=25
40 REM
```

Again if line 35 won't work you could direct the program to say 38 if B=7 where C is assigned the value 25; an extra line say 36 GOTO 40 would also be required for cases where B was not equal to 7.

Sinclair BASIC

Sinclair's BASIC is fairly standard but there are a few strange variations which need explaining to non-Sinclair programmers.

Probably the strangest deviation is in string handling. For example suppose we have

100 LET A$="A STRING OF TEXT"

To pick out the substring STR would require the following expression:

A$(3 TO 5)

Commodore BASIC would achieve the same result with the expression:

MID$(A$,3,3)

In the following programs I will endeavour to point out such problem lines and indicate what the Sinclair BASIC is doing so that you can make the appropriate substitutions in your own dialect.

In the BASIC used in the listings a term such as

DIM A$(3,6)

means we have dimensioned 3 string arrays each consisting of 6 characters. Some other BASICs would just use DIM A$(3).
NB Spectrum and other computers with lower and upper case characters should use upper case only for these programs. On Spectrum use CAPS LOCK.

On the ZX81 CLS means clear the screen and SCROLL moves the display up one line on the TV screen. If your computer requires such control functions use the appropriate command on your machine. Machines like the *VIC20* which have automatic scrolling don't require these lines. However, just in case these lines are required by GOTO or GOSUB statements it is safer generally to enter line number followed by REM. Similarly REM statements should not be eliminated entirely as they may be looping points or labels within the program. However, having said that I will try to point out those lines which should not be deleted.

Non *ZX81* users can eliminate lines containing FAST and SLOW again subject to the same safeguards.

Sinclair BASIC differs from many others in requiring GOTO to follow THEN. For example:

100 IF D=5 THEN GOTO 600

Some systems would need:

110 IF D=5 THEN 600

Please note that some computers require up arrow ↑ instead of ** which is used in the printouts for items raised to a power.

Spectrum users might like to keep the programs as written. To obtain SCROLL on this machine use the following:

POKE 23692,255   (see page 175 of manual)

If this scrolls too rapidly try:

POKE 23692,255: PAUSE 35

Sinclair uses STOP to terminate a program; most BASICs require END.

There are other deviations but I haven't used these features.

Cards

As an example of adapting a program consider the program Cards which was given as a programming example in my previous book, "An Introduction to BASIC Programming" Here we had a line:

130 INPUT H$,I$,J$,K$

As some computers don't accept multiple inputs of this type this was rewritten as shown in lines 130—138.

Line 580 which originally read:

580 T=INT(5*RND(1)+1)

in Sinclair BASIC becomes:

580 LET T = INT((RND*5)+1)

Whatever computer you have this line indicates that a random number 1, 2, 3, 4 or 5 is chosen and assigned to the variable T.

The original program also had:

400 IF A$ = "ACE" GOTO 470

In Sinclair BASIC this becomes:

400 IF A$ = "ACE" THEN GOTO 470

Other systems might require:

400 IF A$ = "ACE" THEN 470

NB With all the variable and constant assignments on Sinclair systems you must have the LET statement. Many computers make LET optional.

On looking at the flow chart in retrospect it occurs to me that the program could be modified to make it more compact. The routines that check the scores could be written as FOR/NEXT loops and Q1, Q2 etc. could be replaced by Q(N); similarly R1, R2 etc. could become R(N). Also if the computer chose the 4 cards initially it would mean the removal of the first guest decision box. Well I leave those sort of mods up to you. My main reason for leaving the program as it is, is that I and my friends have used it in this form for several years and it appears bug free. From experience modifications can lead to problems which are not immediately apparent. In short don't mess with something that works OK.

However, if you like experimenting with programs you could try introducing another set of cards for instance 4 deuces. You might also introduce a condition that you must guess the cards correctly within say 15 attempts or the computer wins and prints back the actual cards chosen.

How to Play

This is a game played with the court cards plus the 2 JOKERS. The computer randomly selects 4 cards and deals them face down to four positions. A game would play like this:

RUN
JACK
JACK   (i.e. Players guesses).
JOKER
JOKER
CORRECT POSITION 0 CORRECT CARDS 1
JACK
JACK
JACK
QUEEN
CORRECT POSITION 2 CORRECT CARDS 2
JACK
KING
QUEEN
KING
CORRECT POSITION 0 CORRECT CARDS 2
ACE
JACK
ACE
QUEEN
CORRECT POSITON 1 CORRECT CARDS 2
QUEEN
JACK
QUEEN
QUEEN
CORRECT POSITION 2 CORRECT CARDS 4
QUEEN
QUEEN
JACK

5

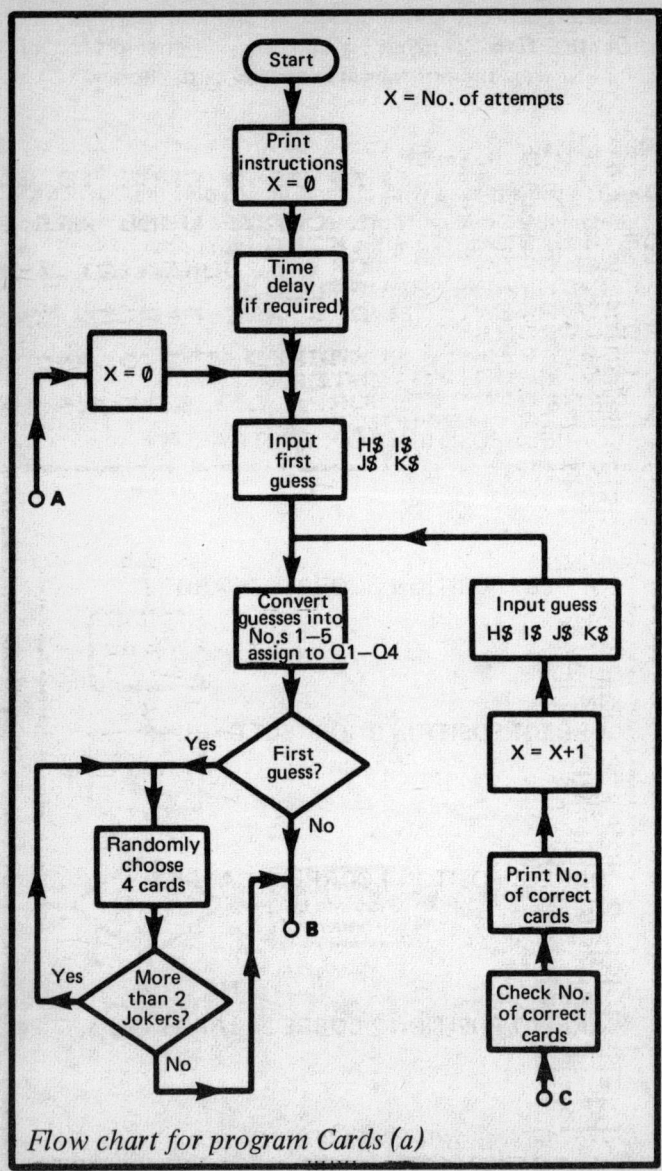

Flow chart for program Cards (a)

QUEEN
CORRECT POSITION 4

(Operator's input underlined)

```
10 LET X=0
25 PRINT "THIS IS A GAME TO GUESS 4 CARDS."
40 PRINT "THE CARDS USED ARE ACE(4),QUEEN(4),KING(4),"
50 PRINT "JACK(4),JOKER(2).THE CARDS ARE SHUFFLED."
55 PRINT "AND 4 ARE PLACED IN POSITIONS"
60 PRINT "NUMBERED 1,2,3 AND 4.YOU HAVE TO ENTER"
70 PRINT "YOUR 4 SELECTIONS UNDER EACH OTHER."
```

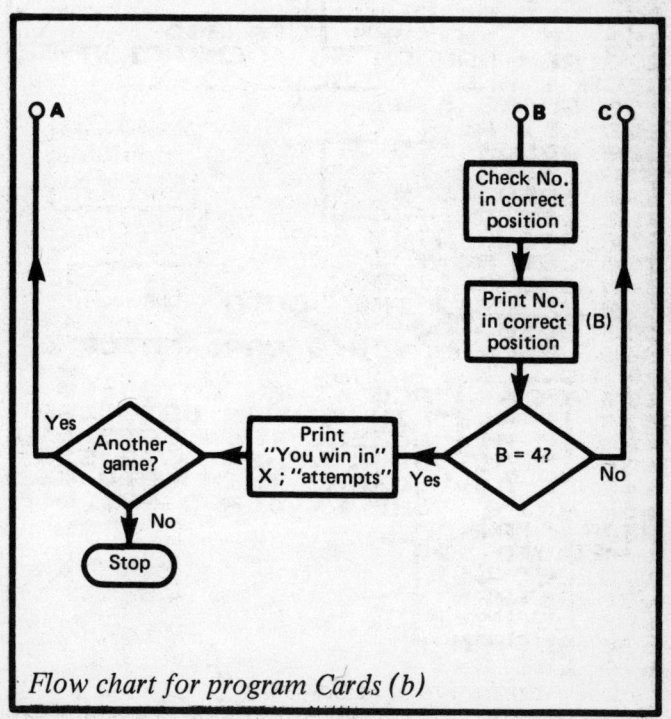

Flow chart for program Cards (b)

```
80 GOSUB 2000
90 GOSUB 2000
120 CLS
125 PRINT "YOU HAVE HAD ";X;" ATTEMPTS"
130 INPUT H$
132 INPUT I$
134 INPUT J$
138 INPUT K$
140 LET A$=H$
150 GOSUB 390
160 LET Q1=C
170 LET A$=I$
180 GOSUB 390
190 LET Q2=C
200 LET A$=J$
210 GOSUB 390
220 LET Q3=C
230 LET A$=K$
240 GOSUB 390
250 LET Q4=C
260 IF X>0 THEN GOTO 600
270 REM RANDOM NO. GENERATOR BETWEEN 1 AND 5 INCL.
280 GOSUB 570
290 LET R1=T
300 GOSUB 570
310 LET R2=T
320 GOSUB 570
330 LET R3=T
340 GOSUB 570
350 LET R4=T
360 GOSUB 1110
370 IF J9>2 THEN GOTO 270
380 GOTO 600
390 REM SUBR-CHKS CARD RETURNS APP NO.
400 IF A$="ACE" THEN GOTO 470
410 IF A$="KING" THEN GOTO 490
420 IF A$="QUEEN" THEN GOTO 510
430 IF A$="JACK" THEN GOTO 530
440 IF A$="JOKER" THEN GOTO 550
450 PRINT "ERROR...CARD NOT DEFINED: ";A$
460 GOTO 120
470 LET C=1
480 RETURN
490 LET C=2
500 RETURN
510 LET C=3
```

```
520 RETURN
530 LET C=4
540 RETURN
550 LET C=5
560 RETURN
570 REM RANDOM NO. GENRATOR
580 LET T=INT ((RND*5)+1)
590 RETURN
600 REM CHKS SCORE...
610 LET B=4
620 IF Q1=R1 THEN GOTO 640
630 LET B=B-1
640 IF Q2=R2 THEN GOTO 660
650 LET B=B-1
660 IF Q3=R3 THEN GOTO 680
670 LET B=B-1
680 IF Q4=R4 THEN GOTO 700
690 LET B=B-1
700 PRINT "NO. IN CORRECT POSITION= ";B
710 LET X=X+1
720 IF B=4 THEN GOTO 1030
730 LET Z=0
740 REM CHKS SCORE NO. RIGHT ANY ORER...
750 LET Y=R1
760 GOSUB 850
770 LET Y=R2
780 GOSUB 850
790 LET Y=R3
800 GOSUB 850
810 LET Y=R4
820 GOSUB 850
830 PRINT "NO. CORRECT CARDS= ";Z
840 GOTO 120
850 REM SUBR CHKS ANY ORDER SCORE...
860 IF Y=Q1 THEN GOTO 910
870 IF Y=Q2 THEN GOTO 940
880 IF Y=Q3 THEN GOTO 970
890 IF Y=Q4 THEN GOTO 1000
900 RETURN
910 LET Z=Z+1
920 LET Q1=0
930 RETURN
940 LET Z=Z+1
950 LET Q2=0
960 RETURN
970 LET Z=Z+1
```

```
 980 LET Q3=0
 990 RETURN
1000 LET Z=Z+1
1010 LET Q4=0
1020 RETURN
1030 PRINT
1040 PRINT "OK YOU WIN IN ";X;" ATTEMPTS"
1050 LET X=0
1060 PRINT
1070 PRINT "DO YOU WANT ANOTHER GAME?ANS YES OR NO:"
1080 INPUT S$
1090 IF S$="YES" THEN GOTO 120
1100 STOP
1110 REM SUBR CHKS ONLY 2 JOKERS CHOSEN.
1120 LET J9=0
1130 IF R1<>5 THEN GOTO 1150
1140 LET J9=J9+1
1150 IF R2<>5 THEN GOTO 1170
1160 LET J9=J9+1
1170 IF R3<>5 THEN GOTO 1190
1180 LET J9=J9+1
1190 IF R4<>5 THEN GOTO 1210
1200 LET J9=J9+1
1210 RETURN
2000 REM SUBR TO DELAY SCREEN CLR...
2050 REM DELAY...
2100 FOR W=1 TO 200
2200 LET D7=0
2300 LET D7=D7+1
2400 NEXT W
2600 RETURN
```

(N.B. Spectrum users require 835 GOSUB 2000)

Biorythms

This program was also listed in my previous book but as it required some major changes to run on the Sinclair computers I thought it useful to list again as it is a very popular program.

The main problem with the Sinclair adaptation is that we are limited to a screen width of 32 characters. If we wish to analyse the graphical print-out we are also limited by the number of lines of output that the screen can accommodate (22). Because of this the present program limits the number of days to 6 (see line 180).

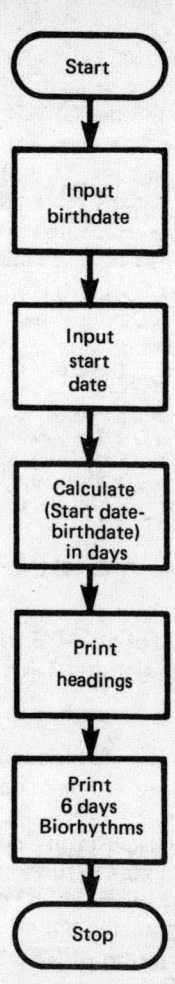

Flow chart for Biorhythm program

In order to view more of the biorhythm print-out you could display 6 days then re-run the program for the next 6 days and so on. Alternatively you could display 6 days then make the program delay for a given period before showing the next 6 days. (Time delays using loops or PAUSE on Sinclair are shown elsewhere in this book.)

I give a fairly simple flow chart for this program since it is easy to follow the actual code. Lines 10–170 input the birth date and the date to start the plots. Line 180 determines the number of days displayed. Lines 190–420 calculate the number of days from birth date to start date. This latter calculation is complex but I think it is all standard BASIC found on most machines. The CLS in line 420 clears the television screen and can be omitted on auto scrolling computers.

A typical run sequence might be:

```
RUN
 29  ⎫
  4  ⎬   (29th April 1959 = birth date.)
 59  ⎭
  1  ⎫
  3  ⎬   (1st March 1983 = Start date.)
 83  ⎭
```

The computer should print: AGE IN DAYS=8708 followed by the biorhythm prediction for March 1st – March 6th 1983.

∗=Physical well being; + = emotional; $ = intellectual.

The display moves from low to high across the screen from left to right and increasing date as it goes down the screen.

```
  5 REM BIORHYTHMS PROGRAM...
 10 PRINT "BIRTHDAY?...EG:"
 30 PRINT "3JUNE1960="
 40 PRINT "3"
 50 PRINT "6"
 60 PRINT "60"
 70 PRINT "?"
 80 INPUT J1
 90 PRINT "?"
100 INPUT J2
110 PRINT "?"
```

```
120 INPUT J3
130 PRINT "LIKEWISE START:"
140 PRINT "?"
150 INPUT J4
160 INPUT J5
170 INPUT J6
180 LET D=6
190 IF J2>2 THEN GOTO 240
200 LET R=(J3-1)*365.25
210 LET R1=INT (R)
220 LET Z1=((J2+12)+1)*30.6
230 GOTO 270
240 LET R=J3*365.25
250 LET R1=INT (R)
260 LET Z1=(J2+1)*30.6
270 LET O=INT (Z1)
280 LET U=O+R1
290 LET U=U+J1
300 IF J5>2 THEN GOTO 350
310 LET R9=(J6-1)*365.25
320 LET R8=INT (R9)
330 LET Z9=((J5+12)+1)*30.6
340 GOTO 380
350 LET R9=J6*365.25
360 LET R8=INT (R9)
370 LET Z9=(J5+1)*30.6
380 LET O2=INT (Z9)
390 LET U1=O2+R8
400 LET U1=U1+J4
410 LET K=(U1-U)+1
420 CLS
430 PRINT "AGE IN DAYS=";K
440 PRINT "BIORYTHM PREDICTION:"
450 PRINT "LOW                  HIGH"
460 PRINT "KEY: PHYS=* EMO=+ INT=$"
470 FOR N=1 TO D
480 LET L=14*SIN (6.284*(N+K)/23)
490 LET L=14+L
500 PRINT TAB L;"*"
510 LET L=14*SIN (6.284*(N+K)/28)
520 LET L=L+14
530 PRINT TAB L;"+"
540 LET L=14*SIN (6.284*(N+K)/33)
550 LET L=L+14
```

```
 560 PRINT TAB L;"$"
 570 NEXT N
9999 STOP
```

```
AGE IN DAYS=8708
BIORYTHM PREDICTION:
LOW                          HIGH
KEY: PHYS=*  EMO=+  INT=$
 *
                $              +
*
                   $              +
*
                      $              +
  *
                        $              +
    *
                           $              +
      *
                              $
```

Chapter 2

CARD GAMES

Shuffle

This program as it stands shuffles the deck of 52 playing cards and deals 10. To deal some other number of cards change lines 10 and 15 as required. For non-Sinclair users line 10 will usually be W$(10). In Sinclair BASIC line 10 dimensions a character array of 10 words each of 9 characters.

Line 35 chooses a random number between 1 and 13 and assigns it to Z Similarly line 45 assigns a random number in the range 1—4 to Y. On another system this might be written:

Y = INT(4*RND(1)+1).

Each card chosen is stored in W$. The program can therefore check if a given card has already been dealt. If it has, it chooses another for that particular value of Q. (Q counts the number of cards dealt.)

Line 76 in Sinclair BASIC means assign the Zth character of A$ to O$ in some BASICs this might be translated as O$=MID$(A$,Z 1). Similarly line 80 means take the substring of C$ starting at the Kth character and ending at the (K+5)th and assign it to L$. Again on some systems we would have:

80 LET L$=MID$(C$, K, 6)

Some machines even provide graphic characters for diamonds, hearts etc. I leave you to adapt my programs to use these.

```
   1 REM   PROG...SHUFFLE
  10 DIM   W$(10,9)
  15 FOR   Q=1 TO 10
  35 LET   Z=INT ((RND*13)+1)
  45 LET   Y=INT ((RND*4)+1)
  50 LET   A$="1234567891JQK"
  60 LET   B$="         QKNG"
  65 LET   C$="CLUBS DMNDS HEARTSS
PADES"
  70 LET   K=(6*Y)-5
```

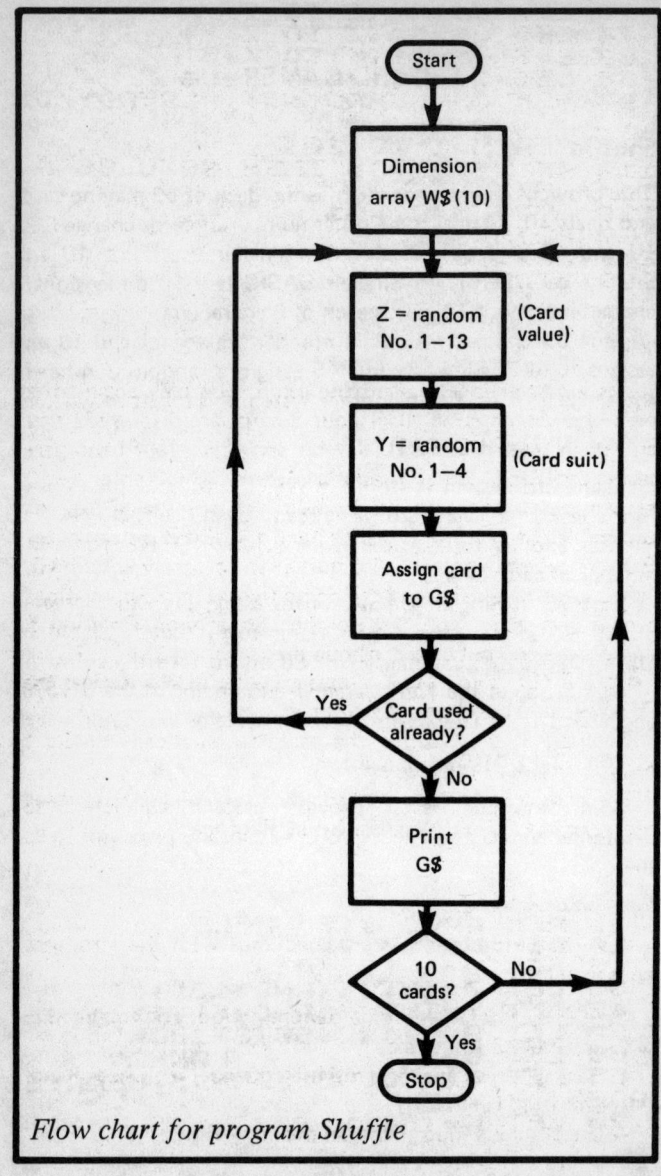

Flow chart for program Shuffle

```
 76 LET O$=A$(Z TO Z)
 78 LET J$=B$(Z TO Z)
 80 LET L$=C$(K TO K+5)
 85 LET G$=O$+J$+" "+L$
 90 REM CHK CARD NOT ALREADY DEALT.
100 FOR N=1 TO 10
110 IF W$(N)=G$ THEN GOTO 35
120 NEXT N
130 LET W$(Q)=G$
190 PRINT G$
200 NEXT Q
9999 STOP
```

Brag

This is a version of the gambling game. You play against the computer. On entering RUN your 3 cards are displayed. You can bet in units of 1 to 10. If you don't like your hand you may enter 0 and lose your ante of 1 unit. If you enter 1—10 the computer will respond by raising you, seeing you or quitting. To see your opponent's hand and end this hand enter 99 at the prompt. You can also quit at any stage by entering 0.

After the hand is played the computer prints your winnings to date and asks if you wish to continue playing. Entering Y prompts the computer to continue the game.

On a *ZX81* if you get a 5 message enter CONT to clear the TV screen and continue the print-out.

Entering Y to continue the game automatically enters 1 into the ante for both players.

The computer is not a particularly strong player but I leave it to your ingenuity to increase his intelligence.

Notes on Brag Version Used

In this version the hands are valued thus with the strongest hands listed first:

1. Pryle = 3 cards of the same denomination. The top hand is 3 Aces, next 3 Kings, etc.
2. A Run. This means 3 cards in sequence, e.g. Ace, King, Queen beats 10, 9, 8.
   Note a Running Flush beats an ordinary Run.

3. A Flush. This means 3 cards of the same suit. If both hands have a Flush the highest card settles it.
4. Pair = 2 cards of the same denomination. For example a pair of Aces beats a pair of Jacks etc.
5. Highest Card. In unmatched hands the highest card wins, e.g. an Ace beats a Jack high etc.

Obviously the logic employed in this program could be extended to Poker but I leave that as an exercise for the reader.

Note the scoring system adopted here reduces the number of programming lines considerably over a method that compared the actual cards.

Program Description

The program utilises two subroutines given elsewhere in this book. The Shuffle routine already listed and the number sort routine (described later).

Please note that line 3 must be included. If not using a *ZX81* just having 3 REM will be sufficient as line 3 is a looping point.

Initially T the winnings (or losses) are set to zero. A, the amount bet by the player is set to zero. The character array M$(3,9) or M$(3) for non-Sinclair users, stores the players's cards. The array Q$(3,9) or Q$(3) stores the computer's cards. Array W$(6) stores all the cards dealt to prevent the same card appearing twice.

The shuffle program randomly chooses the player's hand. The rank of each card 1—13 is assigned to Z and the suit 1—4 is assigned to Y. Initially the 3 values assigned to Z are each stored in the array Z(3) and the first 3 values of Y are stored in B(3)

The number sort routine sorts Z(1), Z(2) and Z(3) into numerical order, lowest first and puts the resultant sorted sequence into array C(3) The program now enters the quality of the hand routine and the counters S1 and X1 are set to zero. Initially the value of the hand is calculated by multiplying the highest card value by 10,000 the next highest by 100 and adding resultants to the lowest card value. This is assigned to S1. (i.e. Using a numbering system based on powers of 100.)

If we have 3 cards the same, for example 3 tens, then 10,000,000 is added to S1. If we have a run 5,300,000 is added to S1. If there is a flush then 4,500,000 is added to S1. For a pair 50,000 X (the value of middle card) is added to S1.

Now if any card is an ace its value is changed from 1 to 13 and the sequence of C(3) rearranged accordingly. The value of S1 is stored in X1 and S1 is then set to zero. The above scoring procedure is repeated. If S1 after this process is less than X1 the old value of S1 is restored.

On returning from the subroutine the score value S1 is stored in P1 for the player's hand. A similar procedure is then followed for the computer's hand and the resultant S1 is stored in P2.

For descriptions of the shuffle and sort routines see appropriate sections of this book.

The computer now displays the player's hand and asks if he wishes to bet in which case he enters his bet in the range 1—10. If he doesn't like his hand he can quit by entering 0. The program then subtracts 1 from T (1 for his ante) and gives him another hand if requested to do so.

The player's bet or raise is stored in variable D. The variable A keeps track of his total stake. H2 tracks the computer's stake.

After the initial bet the player is given the option of seeing the computer's hand. If he does this his stake is raised to that of the computer and the 2 hands are compared and T subsequently adjusted.

The computer computes P2/10,000,000 and assigns the result to H which is a measure of the quality of its hand. If H is less than 1 the computer quits and T=T+H2. H1 is calculated from H to provide an integer number. To "bluff" his opponent the computer chooses a random number between 1 and H1 (inclusive) and assigns this to H1. This value of H1 is used to raise the stake.

If D is too large the computer quits. If the computer's total stake is over 15 he "sees" the opponents hand.

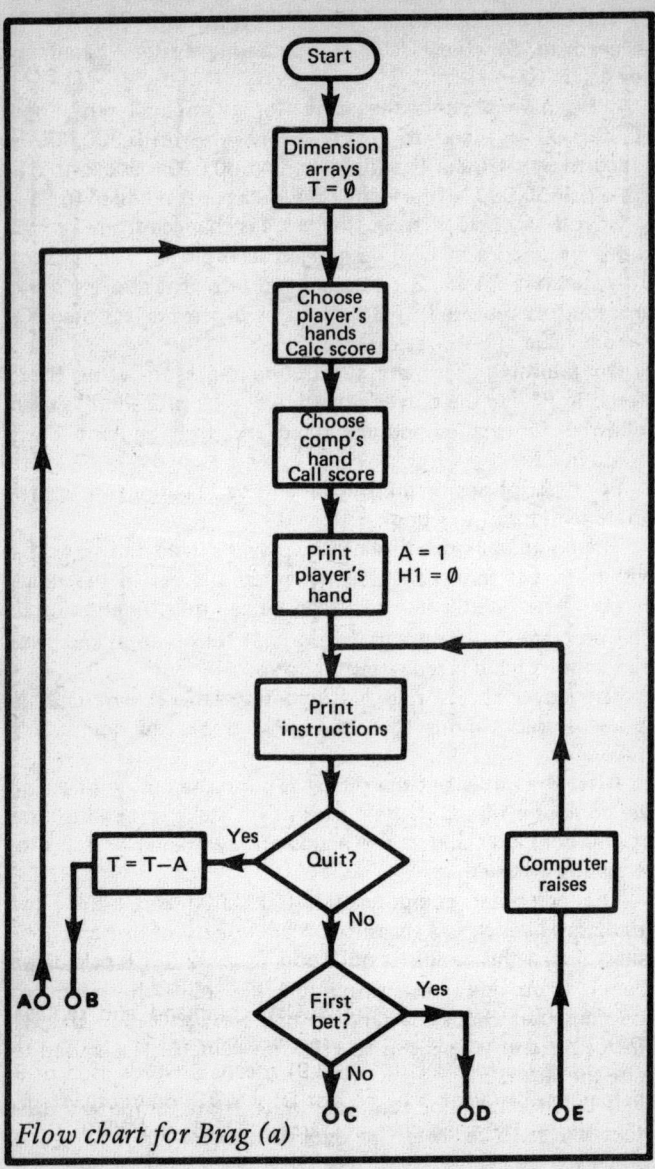

Flow chart for Brag (a)

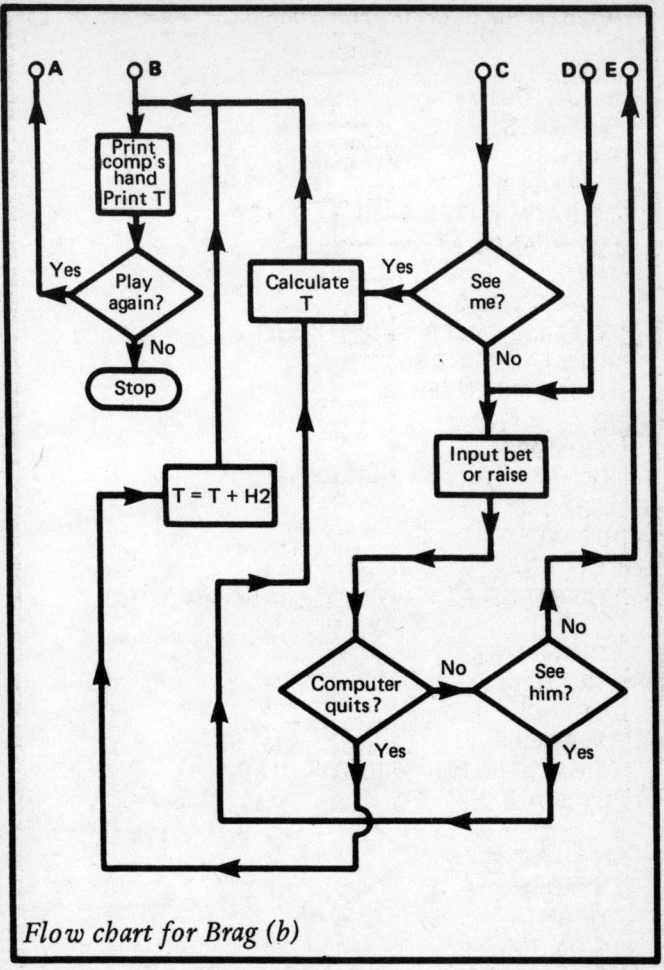

Flow chart for Brag (b)

Spectrum users leave out SLOW command and replace line 3 by 3 REM. Non-Sinclair users do likewise.

Character arrays : DIM M$(3,9) means 3 words each of 9 characters this might become just DIM M$(3) on your system. Similarly for the other character arrays: Q$(3) and W$(3).

A typical run of the Brag program might be:

```
RUN
YOUR HAND =
3 HEARTS
6 CLUBS
2 HEARTS
TO RAISE ENTER 1-10 TO QUIT 0:
POT STANDS AT : 2
1
I RAISE YOU 2
TO RAISE ENTER 1-10 TO QUIT 0 :
POT STANDS AT 6
TO SEE ME ENTER 99
99
YOU LOSE
MY HAND=
3 SPADES
10 SPADES
9 CLUBS
YOU STAND AT : -4 PLAY AGAIN ANS Y/N
Y
YOUR HAND =
8 HEARTS
JK CLUBS
6 SPADES
TO RAISE ENTER 1-10 TO QUIT 0:
POT STANDS AT: 2
0
MY HAND =
2 SPADES
2 HEARTS
KG DMNDS
YOU STAND AT : -5 PLAY AGAIN ANS Y/N
Y
YOUR HAND =
9 CLUBS
7 CLUBS
6 HEARTS
```

```
TO RAISE ENTER 1—10 TO QUIT 0 :
POT STANDS AT : 2
1
I RAISE YOU 2
TO RAISE ENTER 1—10 TO QUIT 0:
POT STANDS AT : 6
TO SEE ME ENTER 99
99
YOU LOSE
MY HAND =
4 SPADES
7 SPADES
KG CLUBS
YOU STAND AT : —9 PLAY AGAIN ANS Y/N
Y
YOUR HAND =
KG HEARTS
10 CLUBS
JK DMNDS
TO RAISE ENTER 1—10 TO QUIT 0 :
POT STANDS AT : 2
2
I RAISE YOU 1
TO RAISE ENTER 1—10 TO QUIT 0 :
POT STANDS AT : 7
TO SEE ME ENTER 99
99
YOU LOSE
MY HAND =
2 SPADES
5 HEARTS
1 CLUBS
YOU STAND AT : —13 PLAY AGAIN ANS Y/N
N
STOP
          (Operator's input underlined)
```

```
   1 REM BRAG....
   2 LET T=0
   3 FAST
   4 LET A=0
   5 LET H1=0
   6 DIM M$(3,9)
   8 DIM Q$(3,9)
  10 DIM W$(6,9)
  20 DIM B(3)
  30 DIM C(3)
  40 DIM Z(3)
  45 CLS
  50 REM DEAL MY HAND...
  55 LET Q=0
  60 FOR J=1 TO 3
  70 GOSUB 1000
  80 LET M$(J)=G$
  90 LET Z(J)=Z
  95 LET B(J)=Y
 100 NEXT J
 105 GOSUB 2000
 107 LET P1=S1
 110 REM PICK COMPS HAND..
 120 FOR J=1 TO 3
 130 GOSUB 1000
 140 LET Q$(J)=G$
 150 LET Z(J)=Z
 160 LET B(J)=Y
 170 NEXT J
 175 GOSUB 2000
 180 LET P2=S1
 190 SLOW
 195 LET A=1
 200 PRINT "YOUR HAND="
 205 LET H2=1
 210 FOR N=1 TO 3
 220 PRINT M$(N)
 230 NEXT N
 233 PRINT "TO RAISE ENTER 1-10 TO QUIT 0:"
 235 PRINT "POT STANDS AT:";A+H2
 238 IF A=1 THEN GOTO 245
 240 PRINT "TO SEE ME ENTER 99"
 245 INPUT D
 248 LET A=A+D
 250 IF D=0 THEN GOTO 945
 255 LET A=A+H1
 260 IF D=99 THEN LET A=A-99
 270 IF D=99 THEN GOTO 500
 280 LET H=P2/1000000
```

```
290 IF H<.1 THEN PRINT "I QUIT.."
300 IF H<.1 THEN GOTO 530
310 LET H1=INT (H/2)
320 LET H1=INT ((RND*H1)+1)
330 IF D>2*H1 THEN PRINT "I QUIT..."
340 IF D>2*H1 THEN GOTO 530
350 IF H>10 THEN LET H=10
360 LET H2=H2+H1+D
370 IF H2>15 THEN PRINT "ILL SEE YOU:"
380 IF H2>15 THEN GOTO 500
390 PRINT "I RAISE YOU ";H1
400 GOTO 233
500 IF P1>P2 THEN PRINT "YOU WIN "
510 IF P2>P1 THEN PRINT "YOU LOSE "
520 IF P1=P2 THEN PRINT "DRAW"
525 GOTO 550
530 LET T=T+H2
540 GOTO 600
550 LET T=T+(SGN (P1-P2))*A
600 REM
800 GOTO 950
945 LET T=T-A
950 PRINT "MY HAND="
960 FOR N=1 TO 3
970 PRINT Q$(N)
980 NEXT N
985 PRINT "YOU STAND AT: ";T;" PLAY AGAIN ANS Y/N"
990 INPUT V$
995 IF V$="Y" THEN GOTO 3
999 GOTO 9999
1000 REM PROG...SHUFFLE
1010 LET Q=Q+1
1020 LET Z=INT ((RND*13)+1)
1030 LET Y=INT ((RND*4)+1)
1050 LET A$="1234567891JQK"
1060 LET B$="         0KNG"
1065 LET C$="CLUBS DMNDS HEARTSSPADES"
1070 LET K=(6*Y)-5
1076 LET O$=A$(Z TO Z)
1078 LET J$=B$(Z TO Z)
1080 LET L$=C$(K TO K+5)
1090 LET G$=O$+J$+" "+L$
1100 GOSUB 1500
```

25

```
1200 RETURN
1500 REM CHK IF CARD ALREADY DELT.
1520 FOR N=1 TO 6
1530 IF W$(N)=G$ THEN GOTO 1020
1550 NEXT N
1570 LET W$(Q)=G$
1600 RETURN
2000 REM SORT PROCEDURE...
2010 LET N1=3
2050 REM INITIALISE COUNTERS.
2060 LET R1=0
2070 DIM F(3)
2100 LET K=0
2400 LET Q7=1
2420 LET Q7=Q7+1
2440 IF Q7=N1+1 THEN GOTO 3000
2450 IF N1=1 THEN GOTO 2500
2460 IF R1=Z(Q7-1) THEN GOTO 2500
2470 LET Q7=Q7-1
2500 LET L=Q7
2520 LET R1=Z(Q7)
2530 IF F(Q7)=1 THEN GOTO 2980
2700 FOR U=1 TO N1
2800 IF F(U)=1 THEN GOTO 2930
2900 IF R1<=Z(U) THEN GOTO 2930
2910 LET R1=Z(U)
2920 LET L=U
2930 NEXT U
2940 LET K=K+1
2950 LET C(K)=R1
2960 LET F(L)=1
2980 GOTO 2420
3000 REM CALC QUALITY OF HAND.
3003 LET X1=0
3005 LET S1=0
3010 LET S1=C(3)*10000+C(2)*100+C(1)
3020 IF C(1)=C(3) THEN LET S1=S1+10000000
3030 IF C(1)+1=C(2) AND C(2)+1=C(3) THEN LET S1=S1+5300000
3040 IF B(1)=B(2) AND B(2)=B(3) THEN LET S1=S1+4500000
3050 IF C(1)=C(2) THEN LET S1=S1+C(2)*150000
3060 IF C(2)=C(3) THEN LET S1=S1+C(2)*150000
3070 IF C(1)<>1 THEN GOTO 3450
```

```
3080 LET C(1)=C(2)
3090 LET C(2)=C(3)
3100 LET C(3)=14
3120 LET X1=S1
3400 GOTO 3005
3450 IF X1>S1 THEN LET S1=X1
3500 REM
5200 RETURN
9999 STOP
```

Pontoon (also known as Blackjack and Vingt et Un)

In this version of the gambling game the computer acts as banker throughout. You are dealt 2 cards and requested if you want another card (twist) or not (stick). There is no limit to the number of cards that you or the banker may draw. In this system of rules a 5 card trick has no significance.

If you are dealt a "Pontoon" i.e. a 10 or court card with an Ace, the banker can only beat you by also drawing a "Pontoon". The Court cards count 10, the Ace counts 1 or 11. If you or the banker scores over 21 the hand is bust and is a loser.

The banker wins if he scores the same number as you or more. Otherwise you win. Even though you may be bust the program still prompts for twist (1) or stick (0) and obviously you would have to enter 0 in this case. This was done to standardise the output on the screen. The program can easily be adjusted to have an automatic exit for M greater than 21 if required.

After a hand is finished the program prompts for you to play again. Answer with a Y if you do. A tally is kept on your winnings or otherwise, 1 point per hand.

The above system approximates to Casino rules.

A typical run of the Pontoon program might be:

<u>RUN</u>
YOUR CARDS:
4 SPADES
7 CLUBS

```
STICK=0 ; TWIST=1
1
KG SPADES
STICK=0 ; TWIST=1
0
YOUR SCORE = 21
MY CARDS:
QN DMNDS
1 SPADES
MY SCORE = 21
YOU LOSE
YOU STAND AT : −1
PLAY AGAIN? ANS Y FOR YES N FOR NO :
Y
YOUR CARDS:
3 HEARTS
8 CLUBS
STICK=0 ; TWIST=1
1
1 DMNDS
STICK=0 ; TWIST=1
0
YOUR SCORE = 12
MY CARDS :
4 HEARTS
8 DMNDS
4 SPADES
9 CLUBS
MY SCORE =25
IM BUST YOU WIN
YOU STAND AT : 0
PLAY AGAIN? ANS Y FOR YES N FOR NO :
N
STOP
```
(Operator's input underlined)

The Pontoon Flow Chart

The flow chart is fairly self explanatory. The variables used in the program are as follows:

T=Winnings or losses to date
F=Flag to record aces. Each time an ace is drawn F=F+1. Reset to zero for computer's hand.
Q=Number of cards dealt
M=Player's score (Maximum legal value =21)
S=Computer's score
W$(24) — Keeps record of all cards dealt
M$(12) — Stores cards dealt to player
S$(12) — Stores cards dealt to computer
V — Variable receives stick (0) or twist (1) value

For those working from the flow chart in order to write a new program (possibly in another language) the flow chart incorporates an improvement. The player's hand if bust exits without requesting STICK/TWIST. I've stuck with the listed version that I've had for sometime.

Program Notes

As before non-Sinclair people will probably require W$(24), M$(12) and S$(12). On *Spectrum* and other auto scrolling machines line 140 can be left out. Lines 480 and 490 — use appropriate random number generator statements as discussed previously (see Shuffle).

Line 9999 is usually END in most BASICs.

I think the program runs fast enough but some *ZX81* users might like a FAST statement at say line 45.

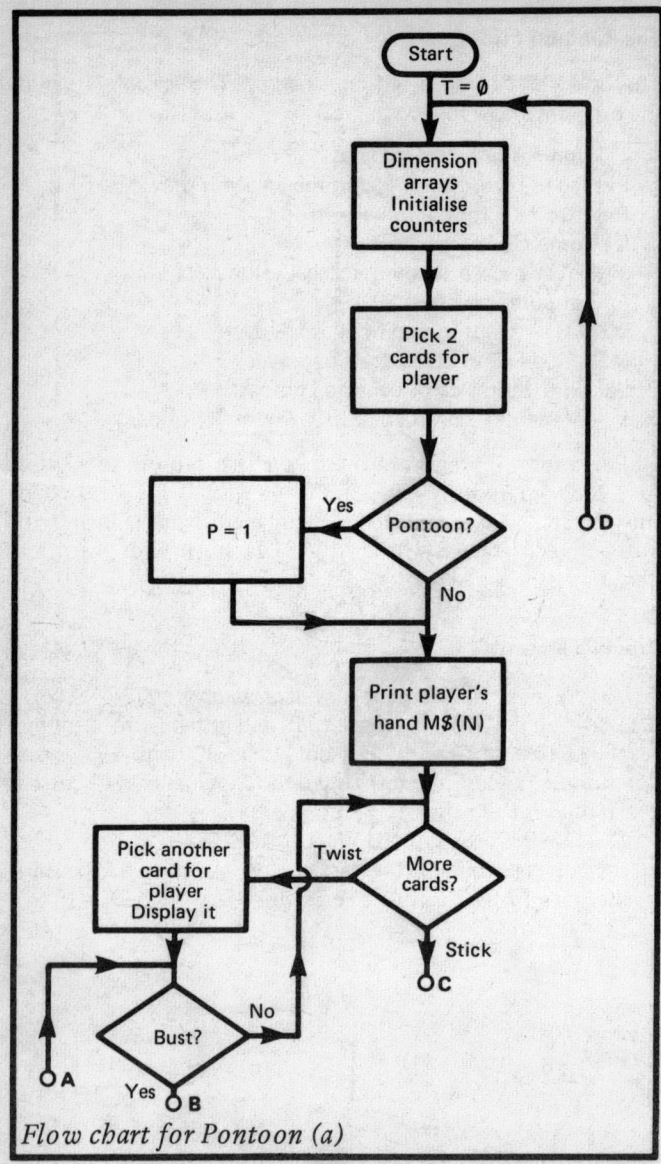

Flow chart for Pontoon (a)

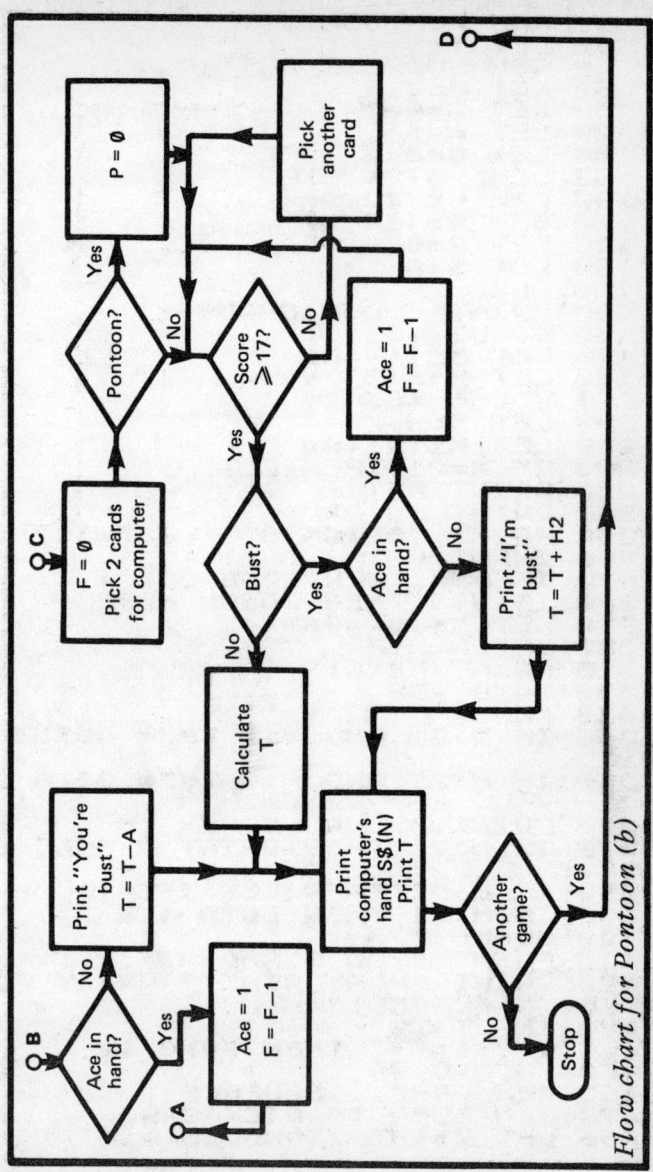

Flow chart for Pontoon (b)

```
1 REM PONTOON....
30 LET T=0
40 REM LOOPING POINT...
50 LET F=0
60 LET Q=0
70 LET M=0
80 LET G=0
90 DIM W$(24,9)
100 DIM M$(12,9)
110 DIM S$(12,9)
120 LET P=0
130 LET S=0
140 CLS
150 PRINT "YOUR CARDS:"
160 GOSUB 460
170 LET M$(1)=G$
180 LET M=M+Z
190 GOSUB 460
200 LET M=M+Z
210 LET M$(2)=G$
220 IF M=21 THEN LET P=1
230 PRINT M$(1)
240 PRINT M$(2)
250 PRINT "STICK=0; TWIST=1."
260 INPUT V
270 IF V=0 THEN GOTO 330
280 IF V=1 THEN GOSUB 460
290 LET M$(Q)=G$
300 LET M=M+Z
310 PRINT M$(Q)
320 GOTO 250
330 REM
340 IF M>21 AND F>0 THEN GOSUB 720
350 IF M>21 AND F>0 THEN GOTO 330
360 PRINT "YOUR SCORE=";M
370 IF M>21 THEN PRINT "YOURE BUST."
380 IF M>21 THEN LET T=T-1
390 IF M>21 THEN GOTO 410
400 GOSUB 770
410 PRINT "YOU STAND AT: ";T
420 PRINT "PLAY AGAIN? ANS Y FOR YES N FOR NO:"
430 INPUT T$
440 IF T$="Y" THEN GOTO 40
450 GOTO 9999
460 REM PROG...SHUFFLE
470 REM SUBR TO PICK CARD:
480 LET Z=INT ((RND*13)+1)
```

```
490 LET Y=INT ((RND*4)+1)
500 LET A$="1234567891JQK"
510 LET B$="         0KNG"
520 LET C$="CLUBS DMNDS HEARTSSPADES"
530 LET K=(6*Y)-5
540 LET O$=A$(Z TO Z)
550 LET J$=B$(Z TO Z)
560 LET L$=C$(K TO K+5)
570 LET G$=O$+J$+" "+L$
580 GOTO 650
590 IF Z=13 THEN LET Z=10
600 IF Z=12 THEN LET Z=10
610 IF Z=11 THEN LET Z=10
620 IF Z=1 THEN LET Z=11
630 IF Z=11 THEN LET F=F+1
640 RETURN
650 REM CHK IF CARD ALREADY DELT.
660 LET Q=Q+1
670 FOR N=1 TO 10
680 IF W$(N)=G$ THEN GOTO 460
690 NEXT N
700 LET W$(Q)=G$
710 GOTO 590
720 REM SUBR TO CHK IF BUST...
730 IF S>21 AND F>0 THEN LET S=S-10
740 IF M>21 AND F>0 THEN LET M=M-10
750 IF F>0 THEN LET F=F-1
760 RETURN
770 REM PICK BANKS CARDS:
780 LET F=0
790 GOSUB 460
800 LET S$(1)=G$
810 LET S=S+Z
820 GOSUB 460
830 LET S$(2)=G$
840 LET S=S+Z
850 PRINT "MY CARDS:"
860 IF S=21 THEN LET P=0
870 PRINT S$(1)
880 PRINT S$(2)
890 LET H=2
900 IF S>=17 THEN GOTO 970
910 GOSUB 460
920 LET H=H+1
930 LET S$(H)=G$
940 PRINT S$(H)
950 LET S=S+Z
```

```
 960 GOTO 900
 970 IF S>21 THEN GOSUB 720
 980 IF S<17 THEN GOTO 900
 990 IF S>21 AND F>0 THEN GOTO 9
20
1000 PRINT "MY SCORE=";S
1010 IF P=1 AND S=21 THEN LET S=
S-1
1020 IF S>21 THEN PRINT "IM BUST
 YOU WIN."
1030 IF S>21 THEN LET T=T+1
1040 IF S>21 THEN GOTO 1090
1050 IF S>=M THEN PRINT "YOU LOS
E."
1060 IF S>=M THEN LET T=T-1
1070 IF S<M THEN PRINT "OK YOU W
IN"
1080 IF S<M THEN LET T=T+1
1090 RETURN
9999 STOP
```

Chapter 3

MORE GAMES

Battleships

This program simulates the old schoolboy favourite. Instead of a human opponent the computer plays against you. In this version the two enemy fleets are composed of 9 ships contained within an area depicted by a 6x6 matrix.

You are initially asked to input your fleet's positions giving the horizontal coordinate (1–6) and then the vertical coordinate. Thus if you wanted your fleet deployed as:

X		X			
	X		X	X	
		X			
				X	X
					X

Your input coordinates would be
 1,1; 1,3; 2,2; 2,4; 2,5; 4,3; 5,4; 5,5; 6,6
These values are then stored in matrix I.

These positions are unknown to the computer. The computer then randomly chooses its own fleet positions and assigns them to matrix C. Ships are stored as 1's in the matrices; blank positions are zeros.

The computer then prints the current score i.e. the number of enemy ships sunk and the number of your ships sunk. It achieves this by counting the number of 1's in each matrix.

You are then requested for your shot. You give the co-ordinates of the point in the enemy area at which you wish your shot to be fired. Your shots are stored in matrix J. J is printed back before each shot to enable you to see your pattern of shots so far. Each of your shots is also checked against J to ensure you don't use the same shot twice. If a shot succeeds in sinking an enemy vessel the computer changes a 1 to 0 in the appropriate matrix.

After your shot the computer randomly chooses a shot at your fleet. Again if successful a 1 is altered to 0 this time in matrix I. A log of the computer's shots is kept in matrix D to prevent it having the same shot twice.

When 9 ships are sunk on either side the issue is decided and the program exits.

Note lines 380–390. This is a time delay to enable you to have time to read the results so far. These lines can be replaced on the *ZX81* by

   380 PAUSE 500

For longer delays increase the value following the PAUSE statement. *Spectrum* users omit lines 395 and 445.

Notes for Non-Sinclair Users

Remove all screen clear statements (CLS) and use your own equivalent of CLS or SCROLL. Many computers have auto-scrolling so just remove CLS lines. Use time delay loop 380–390 to keep results in view if required.

Obviously use your own random number function. On the *ZX81* line 125 means choose a random number between 1 and 6 inclusive and assign it to the variable X Do likewise in your dialect.

Note that some computers require RANDOMIZE, RAND or something similar before using the RND function. If this applies to your computer please insert this extra line in any program that uses RND otherwise you will probably have the same sequence of numbers repeating itself instead of a series of random numbers.

A typical run of Battleships might be (using the coordinates previously quoted):

```
RUN
GIVE YOUR FLEET POSITIONS:
GIVE HORIZONTAL COORD:
1
GIVE VERTICAL COORD:
1
GIVE HORIZONTAL COORD:
1
.
.
.
.
.
.
GIVE HORIZONTAL COORD :
6
GIVE VERTICAL COORD:
6
NO. OF ENEMY SHIPS SUNK=0
NO. OF YOUR SHIPS SUNK=0
SHOTS TO DATE:
0 0 0 0 0 0
0 0 0 0 0 0
0 0 0 0 0 0
0 0 0 0 0 0
0 0 0 0 0 0
0 0 0 0 0 0
ENTER HORIZ COORD 1–6
1
ENTER VERT COORD 1–6
1
NO. OF ENEMY SHIPS SUNK= 0
NO. OF YOUR SHIPS SUNK =0
SHOTS TO DATE:
1 0 0 0 0 0
0 0 0 0 0 0
```

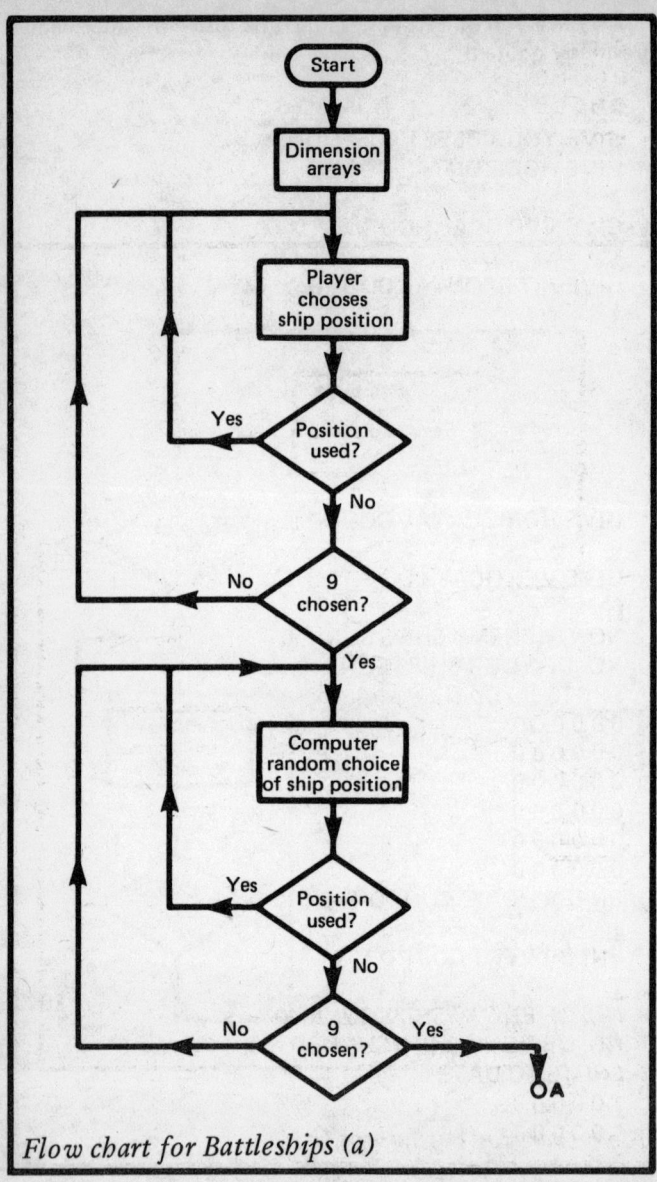

Flow chart for Battleships (a)

```
000000
000000
000000
000000
etc.....
```

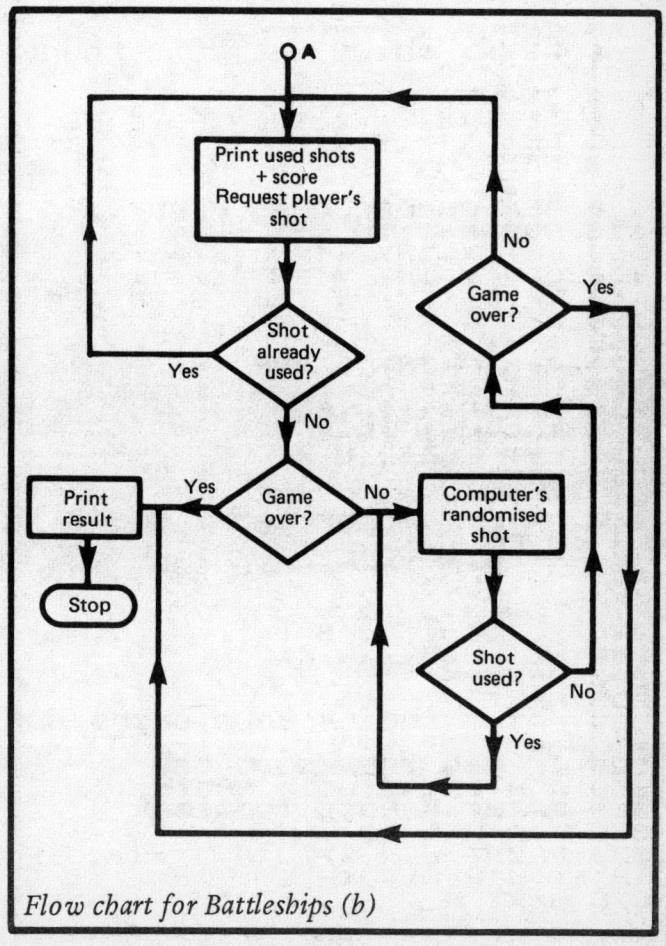

Flow chart for Battleships (b)

```
10 DIM C(6,6)
15 DIM I(6,6)
20 DIM D(6,6)
25 DIM J(6,6)
35 REM PICK YOUR FLEET POSITIO
NS...
40 PRINT "GIVE YOUR FLEET POSI
TIONS:"
45 FOR N=1 TO 9
50 PRINT "GIVE HORIZONTAL COOR
D 1-6:"
55 INPUT X
60 PRINT "GIVE VERTICAL COORD
1-6:"
65 INPUT Y
70 IF I(X,Y)=1 THEN GOTO 50
80 LET I(X,Y)=1
90 NEXT N
95 CLS
110 REM CHOOSE CMPS FLEET...
115 FOR N=1 TO 9
125 LET X=INT ((RND*6)+1)
130 LET Y=INT ((RND*6)+1)
140 IF C(X,Y)=1 THEN GOTO 120
150 LET C(X,Y)=1
155 NEXT N
170 REM PRINT SCORE
205 LET E=0
210 FOR N=1 TO 6
220 FOR K=1 TO 6
225 LET E=E+C(N,K)
230 NEXT K
240 NEXT N
245 PRINT "NO OF ENEMY SHIPS SU
NK=";9-E
250 IF E=0 THEN GOTO 600
260 LET W=0
270 FOR N=1 TO 6
275 FOR K=1 TO 6
280 LET W=W+I(N,K)
290 NEXT K
295 NEXT N
320 PRINT "NO OF YOUR SHIPS SUN
K=";9-W
325 IF W=0 THEN GOTO 600
350 REM PRINT USED SHOTS...
353 PRINT "SHOTS TODATE:"
355 FOR N=1 TO 6
370 PRINT J(N,1);J(N,2);J(N,3);J(N,4);J(N,5);J(N,6)
375 NEXT N
```

```
380 REM TIME DELAY
382 FOR N=1 TO 50
385 LET O=N
390 NEXT N
395 CLS
400 REM ENTER YOUR SHOT...
410 PRINT "ENTER HORIZ COORD 1-
6:"
420 INPUT X
430 PRINT "ENTER VERT COORD 1-6
:"
440 INPUT Y
445 CLS
450 IF J(X,Y)=1 THEN GOTO 480
455 LET J(X,Y)=1
460 LET C(X,Y)=0
470 GOTO 500
480 PRINT "YOUVE USED THAT...."
485 GOTO 400
500 REM CMPS SHOT...
510 RAND
520 LET X=INT ((RND*6)+1)
530 LET Y=INT ((RND*6)+1)
540 IF D(X,Y)=1 THEN GOTO 500
545 LET D(X,Y)=1
550 LET I(X,Y)=0
560 GOTO 170
600 PRINT "END."
610 STOP
```

(Spectrum users omit line 510)

Solitaire

This is the English version of the board game. There are 33 pegs mounted in holes on a board. A peg may jump over an adjacent peg into an empty hole beyond. The peg jumped over is removed. Only horizontal and vertical moves are allowed.

The player endeavours to end up with just 1 peg left on the board. In some versions this peg must be left in the central hole but this computer version does not check this. (This feature can easily be incorporated if required.)

On entering RUN the board is displayed with 1's depicting pegs and 0's holes thus:

```
          1 1 1
          1 1 1
        1 1 1 1 1 1 1
        1 1 1 0 1 1 1
        1 1 1 1 1 1 1
          1 1 1
          1 1 1
```

You are then requested for your move. First you enter the vertical coordinate, then the horizontal coordinate of the peg to be moved. You then enter the coordinates of the space to which the peg is to be moved. The coordinate system used is as shown:

```
                    Horizontal
            1   2   3   4   5   6   7
         ┌───┬───┬───┬───┬───┬───┬───┐
       1 │   │   │   │   │   │   │   │
         ├───┼───┼───┼───┼───┼───┼───┤
       2 │   │   │   │   │   │   │   │
         ├───┼───┼───┼───┼───┼───┼───┤
   V   3 │   │   │   │   │   │   │   │
   e     ├───┼───┼───┼───┼───┼───┼───┤
   r   4 │   │   │   │ 0 │   │   │   │
   t     ├───┼───┼───┼───┼───┼───┼───┤
   i   5 │   │   │   │   │   │   │   │
   c     ├───┼───┼───┼───┼───┼───┼───┤
   a   6 │   │   │   │ X │   │   │   │
   l     ├───┼───┼───┼───┼───┼───┼───┤
       7 │   │   │   │   │   │   │   │
         └───┴───┴───┴───┴───┴───┴───┘
```

Thus to enter the move from X in the diagram to 0, you would enter:

6
4
4
4

This represents the move (6,4) to (4,4).

The computer checks if this is a legal move. If not legal an error message is displayed and you are once more prompted for this move. If the move is legal the new board is displayed and the game continues until no more valid moves remain.

If you cannot solve the puzzle one solution is given in the appendix.

Solitaire Program Notes

The matrix used is a 7X7 i.e. M(7,7). Numbers are initially assigned to matrix elements thus:

```
9 9 1 1 1 9 9
9 9 1 1 1 9 9
1 1 1 1 1 1 1
1 1 1 0 1 1 1
1 1 1 1 1 1 1
9 9 1 1 1 9 9
9 9 1 1 1 9 9
```

The character matrix M$(7,7) or M$(7) is a mirror of the number matrix. The character matrix is used to print out the board. If number matrix element is a 9 then corresponding character matrix element is assigned a space. If there is a 1 or 0 in the number matrix the corresponding character matrix elements get the same character.

The array Z(4) is used to assign "9" values in M(7,7).
F is a flag which is set to 1 for an illegal move.
S is the sum of matrix M(7,7) it equals 145 to win a game.
G is a flag which is set to zero if there are no more legal moves.
X1 = horizontal coord of peg to be moved.
Y1 = vertical coord of peg to be moved.
X2 = horizontal coord of space peg moved to.
Y2 = vertical coord of space peg moved to.

For a legal move conditions 1–4 must be met:
1. |X1–X2| = 2 AND Y1=Y2
    or |Y1–Y2| = 2 AND X1=X2

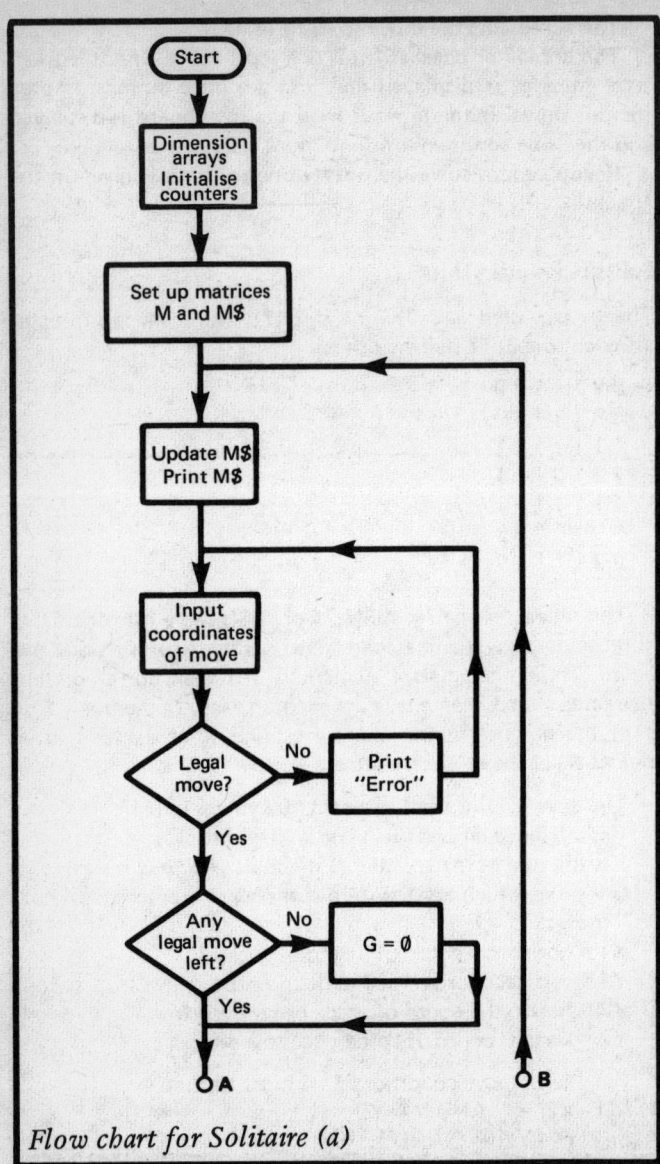

Flow chart for Solitaire (a)

2. M(X1,Y1) = 1
3. M(X2,Y2) = 0
4. M((X1+X2)/2, (Y1+Y2)/2) = 1

```
  1 REM SOLITAIRE...
 30 FAST
 40 LET G=1
 50 DIM M(7,7)
 60 DIM H$(7,7)
 70 DIM Z(4)
 80 FOR N=1 TO 7
 90 FOR K=1 TO 7
100 LET M(N,K)=1
110 NEXT K
120 NEXT N
130 LET M(4,4)=0
```

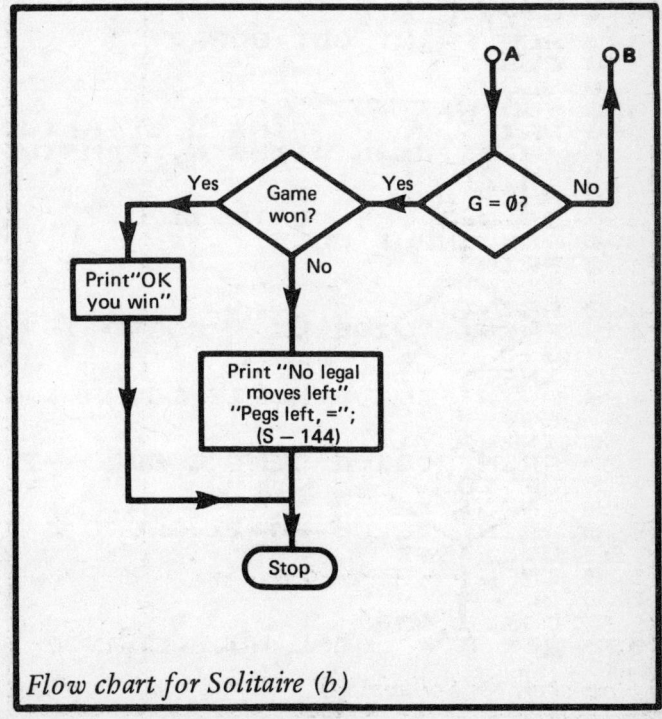

Flow chart for Solitaire (b)

```
140 REM SET NON USED TO 9.
150 LET Z(1)=1
160 LET Z(2)=2
170 LET Z(3)=6
180 LET Z(4)=7
190 FOR N=1 TO 4
200 FOR K=1 TO 4
210 LET M(Z(N),Z(K))=9
220 NEXT K
230 NEXT N
240 REM PREPARE BOARD...
250 FOR N=1 TO 7
260 FOR K=1 TO 7
270 IF M(N,K)=9 THEN LET M$(N,K
)=" "
280 IF M(N,K)=1 THEN LET M$(N,K
)="1"
290 IF M(N,K)=0 THEN LET M$(N,K
)="0"
300 NEXT K
310 NEXT N
320 REM PRINT OUT BOARD..
330 CLS
340 SLOW
350 FOR N=1 TO 7
360 PRINT "        ";M$(N,1);M$(N,
2);M$(N,3);M$(N,4);M$(N,5);M$(N,
6);M$(N,7)
370 NEXT N
380 IF G=0 THEN GOTO 1120
390 REM INPUT MOVE:
400 PRINT
410 PRINT
420 PRINT
430 PRINT "GIVE VERT COORD 1-7
OF PEG:"
440 INPUT X1
450 PRINT "GIVE HORIZ COORD 1-7
OF PEG:"
460 INPUT Y1
470 PRINT "GIVE VERT COORD 1-7
TO MOVE TO:"
480 INPUT X2
490 PRINT "GIVE HORIZ COORD 1-7
TO MOVE TO:"
500 INPUT Y2
510 CLS
520 GOSUB 630
530 REM FOR LEGAL MOVE CHANGE B
OARD.
```

```
540 IF F=1 THEN GOTO 560
550 GOTO 580
560 PRINT "ERROR RE-ENTER:"
570 GOTO 320
580 LET M(X1,Y1)=0
590 LET M(X2,Y2)=1
600 LET M(((X1+X2)/2),((Y1+Y2)/2))=0
610 GOSUB 770
620 GOTO 240
630 REM CHK LEGAL MOVES...
640 IF ABS (X1-X2)=2 AND Y1=Y2 THEN GOTO 680
650 IF ABS (Y1-Y2)=2 AND X1=X2 THEN GOTO 680
660 LET F=1
670 GOTO 760
680 IF M(X1,Y1)=1 AND M(X2,Y2)=0 THEN GOTO 710
690 LET F=1
700 GOTO 760
710 IF M(((X1+X2)/2),((Y1+Y2)/2))=1 THEN GOTO 740
720 LET F=1
730 GOTO 760
740 LET F=0
750 LET G=1
760 RETURN
770 REM SUBR CHK END OF GAME.
780 LET S=0
790 FOR N=1 TO 7
800 FOR K=1 TO 7
810 LET S=S+M(N,K)
820 NEXT K
830 NEXT N
840 IF S=145 THEN PRINT "OK YOU WIN..."
850 IF S=145 THEN GOTO 9999
860 LET G=0
870 REM CHK ANY LEGAL MOVES LEFT...
880 FAST
890 FOR N=1 TO 7
900 FOR K=1 TO 7
910 IF G=1 THEN GOTO 1110
920 LET X1=N
930 LET Y1=K
940 LET X2=N
950 LET Y2=K+2
960 IF Y2>7 THEN GOTO 980
970 GOSUB 630
```

```
 980 LET Y2=K-2
 990 IF Y2<1 THEN GOTO 1010
1000 GOSUB 630
1010 LET X2=N-2
1020 LET Y2=K
1030 IF X2<1 THEN GOTO 1050
1040 GOSUB 630
1050 LET X2=N+2
1060 IF X2>7 THEN GOTO 1080
1070 GOSUB 630
1080 NEXT K
1090 NEXT N
1100 SLOW
1110 RETURN
1120 PRINT
1130 PRINT
1140 PRINT
1150 IF G=0 THEN PRINT "NO LEGAL
 MOVES LEFT * PEGS LEFT=";S-144
9999 STOP
```

(N.B. Spectrum users omit lines 30, 330, 340, 510, 880, 1100)

Calendar

A few years ago I came across someone who performed a singular feat of mental magic. You could quote any date in the twentieth century and he would tell you on which day of the week it occurred. On quizzing him he told me that he had memorized a key number for each year and another for each month. These numbers were added to the day of the month given and the result divided by seven. The remainder gave the required day of the week.

I considered this approach but decided against it when writing this program. That method requires too much data to be stored within the program. Therefore I went back to basics. The main problem is that of deciding which years are leap years.

As it stands the program works from 1753 up to any date in the future based on the Gregorian Calendar. Since writing this program I note that the Sinclair *Spectrum* manual has a program that performs a similar function but as this only applies to the 20th century I hope *Spectrum* users will find my program of interest. In addition my program can be adapted to other problems which I shall explain shortly.

If you only want dates after 1900 and you find the computer response too slow you can change lines 150 and 190 to read 1900 instead of 1753. Please note however, that this only happens to work for 1900. Any other start year will probably require the constant 1 in line 70 to be changed. To find the value to be substituted for 1 in line 70 run the program with replacement year for 1753 and note by how many days the result is out. Then adjust line 70 accordingly.

Variables used:

Y = year; E = day; M$ = month (for input date).
D$ = Day of week
F = flag set to 1 for a leap year.

Test for leap year (see lines 120–135). Year must be exactly divisible by 4 but not 100 unless divisible exactly by 400. Lines 150–180 count leap years between origin and (Y−1). The subroutine starting at line 280 counts the days in given year up to the date given. The total number of days from the origin (1st Jan 1753) to the input date is calculated and assigned to D.

D is divided by 7 and the integer part of it taken. The resultant is multiplied by 7 and subtracted from D. This gives required day of the week as a number. A subroutine converts this number into an actual day which is printed out.

The program could easily be modified to print out several days or a whole month if you have a printer. You could use the fact that the moon's phases recur at 29.5 day intervals to compute on which days the new moon or full moon will occur. Knowing the periods of the planets you could predict in which signs of the zodiac they will appear on a given date.

For dates prior to 1753 they used the Julian Calendar. This calculated a leap year if the year was divisible by 4. The program can thus be simplified to cover dates before 1753. If you know the actual day any date before 1752 fell then you can find the constant required in line 70. Alternatively you could use the fact that in 1752 when they changed systems the old Julian Calendar was +11 days out. Following September 2nd 1752 the next day was 13 September 1752.

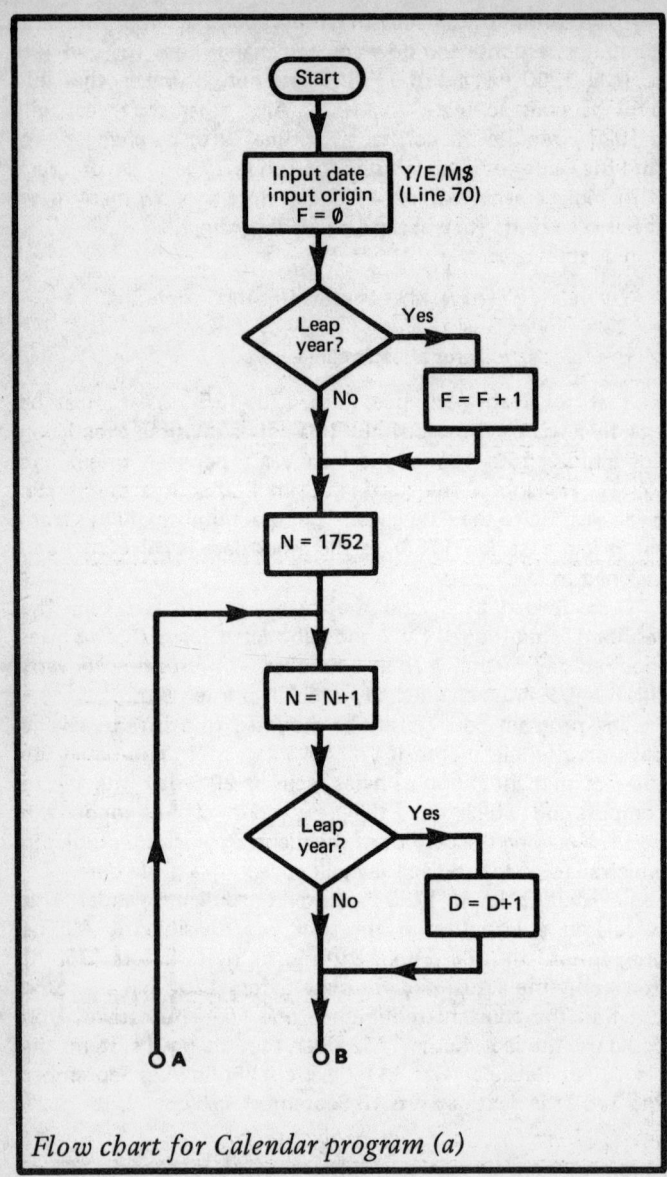

Flow chart for Calendar program (a)

A typical run of Calendar might be:

RUN
GIVE YEAR :
1923
INPUT DAY AS A NUMBER :
2
INPUT MONTH FIRST 3 LETTERS :
JUN
2JUN1923
FELL ON A SATURDAY.

(Operator's input underlined)

```
 1 REM CALENDAR CALCULATOR...
30 PRINT "GIVE YEAR:"
40 INPUT Y
50 PRINT "INPUT DAY AS NUMBER:
..
```

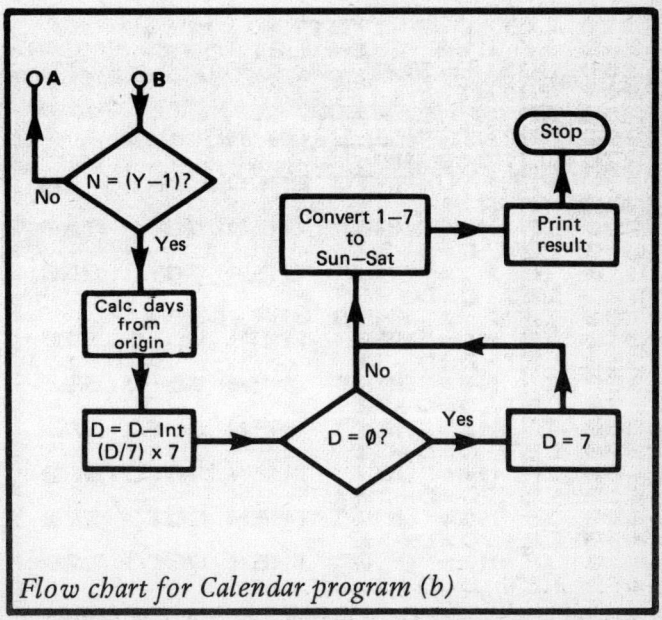

Flow chart for Calendar program (b)

```
  60 INPUT E
  70 LET D=E+1
  80 PRINT "INPUT MONTH FIRST 3
LETTERS:"
  90 INPUT M$
 100 REM CHK FOR LEAP YEAR:
 110 LET F=0
 120 IF (Y/4)-INT (Y/4)=0 THEN L
ET F=1
 130 IF (Y/100)-INT (Y/100)=0 TH
EN LET F=0
 135 IF (Y/400)-INT (Y/400)=0 TH
EN LET F=1
 140 REM ROUTINE TO COUNT NO OF
LEAP YEARS
 150 FOR N=1753 TO Y-1
 160 IF (N/4)-INT (N/4)=0 THEN L
ET D=D+1
 170 IF (N/100)-INT (N/100)=0 TH
EN LET D=D-1
 175 IF (N/400)-INT (N/400)=0 TH
EN LET D=D+1
 180 NEXT N
 190 LET D=D+(Y-1753)*365
 200 GOSUB 260
 210 LET D=D-(INT (D/7))*7
 220 IF D=0 THEN LET D=7
 230 GOSUB 530
 240 PRINT
 250 PRINT E;M$;Y
 260 PRINT "FELL ON A ";D$
 270 GOTO 9999
 280 REM SUBR TO CALC. DAYS IN F
INAL YEAR...
 290 IF M$="JAN" THEN GOTO 520
 300 LET D=D+31
 310 IF M$="FEB" THEN GOTO 520
 320 LET D=D+28
 330 IF F=1 THEN LET D=D+1
 340 IF M$="MAR" THEN GOTO 520
 350 LET D=D+31
 360 IF M$="APR" THEN GOTO 520
 370 LET D=D+30
 380 IF M$="MAY" THEN GOTO 520
 390 LET D=D+31
 400 IF M$="JUN" THEN GOTO 520
 410 LET D=D+30
 420 IF M$="JUL" THEN GOTO 520
 430 LET D=D+31
 440 IF M$="AUG" THEN GOTO 520
 450 LET D=D+31
```

```
460 IF M$="SEP" THEN GOTO 520
470 LET D=D+30
480 IF M$="OCT" THEN GOTO 520
490 LET D=D+31
500 IF M$="NOV" THEN GOTO 520
510 LET D=D+30
520 RETURN
530 REM SUBR TO CONVERT 1-7 TO DAY
540 IF D=1 THEN LET D$="SUNDAY"
550 IF D=2 THEN LET D$="MONDAY"
560 IF D=3 THEN LET D$="TUESDAY"
570 IF D=4 THEN LET D$="WEDNESDAY"
580 IF D=5 THEN LET D$="THURSDAY"
590 IF D=6 THEN LET D$="FRIDAY"
600 IF D=7 THEN LET D$="SATURDAY"
610 RETURN
9999 STOP
```

Chapter 4

SORTING

Alpha Sort Routine

This program demonstrates how one can sort alphanumeric data. Instead of assigning all the data A$(1), A$(2) etc. the data could have been input by an INPUT loop using A$(N) as N = 1 TO 10 for example.

In the sort sequence S$(N) is initially set to "ZZZZZ" which is greater than any probable value of A$(N). S$(N) is compared with each of the data values. If S$(N) is greater than or equal to A$(K) the value of K is stored in variable H and S$(N) is made equal to A$(K). Eventually the lowest value of A$(K) is assigned to S$(N) and the corresponding flag F(H) is set to 1. Thus on each pass for a value of N the lowest value of A$(K) which does not have its corresponding flag F(K) set to 1 is assigned to S$(N). So the sorted data is eventually loaded into S$(1) to S$(10).

To sort your own data just change the assignment statements involving A$(1) to A$(10). Obviously the method can be modified to sort as many items of data as you require depending on the limitations imposed by your computer.

In case some systems won't accept this method I quote a second less elegant system. I think it is self explanatory so no flow chart is provided. The routine compares the data items in turn with AA, AB, AC . . . . BA, BB, BC . . . . etc. down to ZW, ZX, ZY, ZZ If the first two letters of the data item are the same as the two letters the program prints the data. Thus this method only sorts on the first two letters.

Returning to the first of these sort programs it can of course be applied to sorting numbers by replacing S$(10), A$(10) with S(10), A(10) and assigning S(N) = 99999 or some other large number greater than any number likely to be included in the data. A more general method which doesn't require this assignment is listed. As this general method is close to the original alpha sort, no flow chart is provided. This program is used as a subroutine in the earlier program called

Brag.

Please remember to use only capitals. On *Spectrum* for instance to sort upper and lower case data S$(N) should initially be set to "ZZZZZ". On the *Spectrum* upper case characters are sorted before lower case.

```
10 REM ALPHA SORT ROUTINE...
20 DIM F(10)
30 DIM S$(10,10)
40 DIM A$(10,10)
50 LET N=0
55 LET A$(1)="ZEBRA"
60 LET A$(2)="CAMEL"
65 LET A$(3)="CROCODILE"
70 LET A$(4)="DOG"
75 LET A$(5)="SNAKE"
80 LET A$(6)="CHEETAH"
85 LET A$(7)="ARDVARK"
90 LET A$(8)="WHALE"
95 LET A$(9)="HORSE"
100 LET A$(10)="DONKEY"
110 REM SORTING...
115 IF N=10 THEN GOTO 200
120 LET N=N+1
130 LET S$(N)="ZZZZZ"
140 FOR K=1 TO 10
145 IF F(K)=1 THEN GOTO 170
150 IF S$(N)>=A$(K) THEN LET H=K
160 IF S$(N)>=A$(K) THEN LET S$(N)=A$(K)
170 NEXT K
180 LET F(H)=1
190 GOTO 110
200 REM PRINT OUT RESULT..
210 PRINT "SORTED DATA..."
220 FOR N=1 TO 10
230 PRINT S$(N)
240 NEXT N
999 STOP




10 DIM M$(50,12)
20 LET A$="ABCDEFGHIJKLMNOPQRSTUVWXYZ"
30 LET B$=A$
```

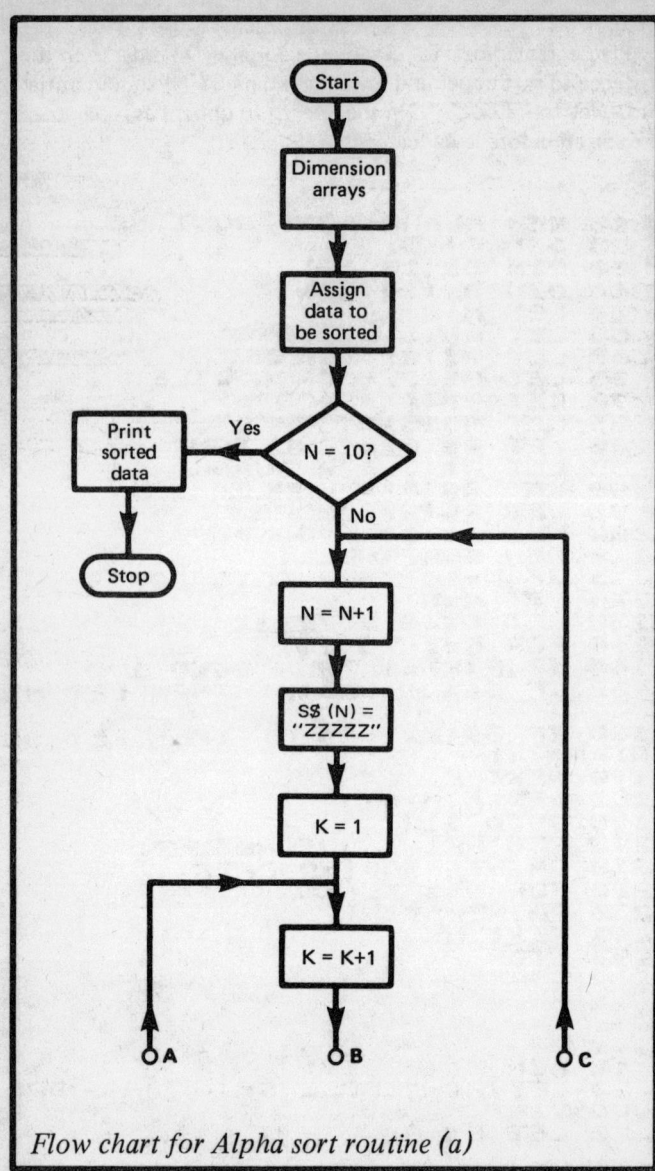

Flow chart for Alpha sort routine (a)

```
40 PRINT "HOW MANY NAMES?"
45 INPUT X
50 PRINT X
55 CLS
60 FOR N=1 TO X
70 PRINT "GIVE VALUE:"
80 INPUT M$(N)
85 PRINT M$(N)
88 CLS
90 NEXT N
100 REM SORT...
101 PRINT "SORTED DATA..."
102 FOR N=1 TO 26
108 FOR K=1 TO 26
110 FOR Z=1 TO X
```

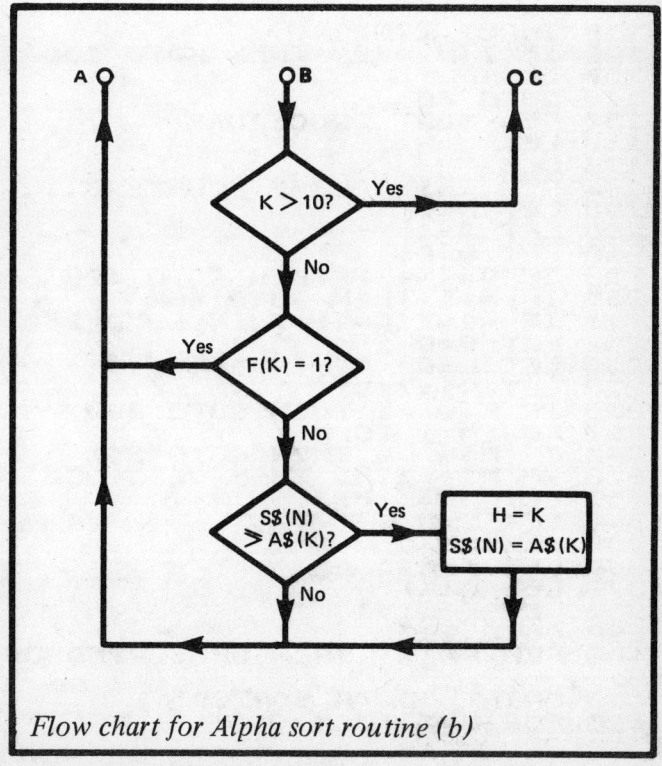

Flow chart for Alpha sort routine (b)

```
140 IF M$(Z,1 TO 2)=(A$(N TO N)
+B$(K TO K)) THEN PRINT M$(Z)
150 NEXT Z
160 NEXT K
180 NEXT N
400 STOP


 10 REM SORT PROG...
 30 LET R1=0
 40 LET N=0
 50 DIM Z(10)
 60 DIM C(10)
 70 DIM F(10)
 80 REM INPUT DATA...
 90 LET N=N+1
100 PRINT "INPUT NO. -99 TO END
"
110 INPUT Z(N)
120 IF Z(N)=-99 THEN GOTO 150
130 CLS
140 GOTO 80
150 REM SORT PROCEDURE
160 LET N=N-1
170 CLS
180 REM INITIALISE COUNTERS...
190 LET K=0
200 LET Q=1
210 LET Q=Q+1
220 IF Q=(N+1) THEN GOTO 400
230 IF N=1 THEN GOTO 260
240 IF R1=Z(Q-1) THEN GOTO 260
250 LET Q=Q-1
260 LET L=Q
270 LET R1=Z(Q)
280 IF F(Q)=1 THEN GOTO 390
290 FOR M=1 TO N
300 IF F(M)=1 THEN GOTO 350
310 IF R1<=Z(M) THEN GOTO 350
330 LET R1=Z(M)
340 LET L=M
350 NEXT M
360 LET K=K+1
370 LET C(K)=R1
380 LET F(L)=1
390 GOTO 210
400 REM PRINT BACK OF SORTED DA
TA...
410 PRINT "DATA SORTED:"
420 FOR U=1 TO N
```

```
430 PRINT C(U)
440 NEXT U
9999 STOP
```

(N.B. The number sort routine requires you to enter −99 to end input. If you wish to sort a set of numbers including the value −99 change line 120. If you know that you won't be sorting the number −999 substitute this value in line 120.

As it stands the number sort routine will only sort up to 10 numbers — see lines 50-70. Change 10 in lines 50, 60, 70 to required value.

Spectrum users can omit CLS lines if they prefer.)

Chapter 5

FILING SYSTEMS

Files

I am going to describe a BASIC system for use on a home computer which is akin to the type of systems that are built into mainframe computers using COBOL. Obviously the main limitation on the small system is the amount of memory available.

The system here in its most powerful form will only work on computers like the Sinclair *Spectrum* and *ZX81* which save your variables and arrays along with the program.

To illustrate the method which you can tailor to your requirements I have chosen to store data on the chemical elements. The fields are as follows

ELEMENT NAME : Up to 12 characters long stored in
   array E$(50,12)
ELEMENT SYMBOL : Up to 2 characters long stored in
   array S$(50,2)
ATOMIC NO. : Up to 2 characters long stored in array
   A$(50,2)
ATOMIC WEIGHT : Up to 3 characters long stored in array
   W$(50,2)

From the dimension statements you can see that we have limited ourselves to 50 records i.e. information on 50 elements. To cover all 92 naturally occurring elements we would require 92 records so the dimension statements would have to be adjusted accordingly.

After building the program you can enter RUN. On being asked for how many records to add you could enter 4. The program will now loop around 4 times requesting the first 4 records. You might enter:

LITHIUM
LI
3
7

HYDROGEN
H
1
1
CARBON
C
6
12
IRON
FE
26
56

You can now save the program straight away onto cassette tape. Now reload the program but *do not enter* RUN. Instead say GOTO 12. If you now enter that you wish to add another 4 records they will be stored as records 5 to 8 (inclusive). Note RUN, NEW, and CLEAR will destroy the records already stored so don't use them whilst you are using this program.

If on adding the further 4 records you SAVE onto tape you will have SAVED the program plus the eight records so far entered. If you say GOTO 105 you will obtain a report of all the records in your data base. GOTO 500 gives you another report in which the elements are sorted alphabetically. Note that I have used the cruder sort routine as it is more universal. Again note that it only sorts on the first two letters. You can obviously improve on the quality and the speed of this sort by utilising the other Alpha sort routine quoted previously. One way of doing this would be to sort the elements into an array say V$(50) — only use up to Kth element — then write a routine that compares V$(J) with each E$(N) where J=1 TO K. On finding equality print out E$(N);S$(N);A$(N);W$(N).

GOTO 600 gives an example of a special report. Here only records in which the atomic weight is greater than 11 are listed.

Note that the variable K which is SAVED each time with the program keeps a tally of the number of records stored to date.

Unfortunately if your computer doesn't SAVE variables

and arrays with your program you can't store your data so elegantly. Your DIM statements will probably be E$(50), S$(50) etc. You will probably have to store your data in DATA statements thus:

700 DATA LITHIUM,LI,3,7
710 DATA HYDROGEN,H 1,1
etc ...

Some systems may require

700 DATA "LITHIUM","LI","3","7"

Lines 12–50 would not be needed. You would add new data by simply adding new DATA lines. Use your substring method for example line 535 might be

535 LET G$ =   MID$(E$(Z),1,2)

```
  1 LET K=0
  3 DIM A$(50,2)
  5 DIM W$(50,3)
  7 DIM S$(50,2)
  8 DIM E$(50,12)
 10 REM FILE SYSTEM...
 12 PRINT "HOW MANY TO ADD:"
 14 INPUT X
 15 FOR N=K+1 TO K+X
 20 PRINT "GIVE ELEMENT:"
 25 INPUT E$(N)
 30 PRINT "GIVE SYMBOL:"
 32 INPUT S$(N)
 35 PRINT "GIVE ATOMIC NO.:"
 40 INPUT A$(N)
 45 PRINT "GIVE ATOMIC WT.:"
 50 INPUT W$(N)
 55 CLS
 60 NEXT N
 70 LET K=N-1
 90 GOTO 1000
105 PRINT "REPORT..."
110 FOR N=1 TO K
120 PRINT E$(N);" ";S$(N);" ";A$(N);" ";W$(N)
130 NEXT N
140 GOTO 1000
500 REM SORTER..
505 PRINT "SORTED REPORT..."
```

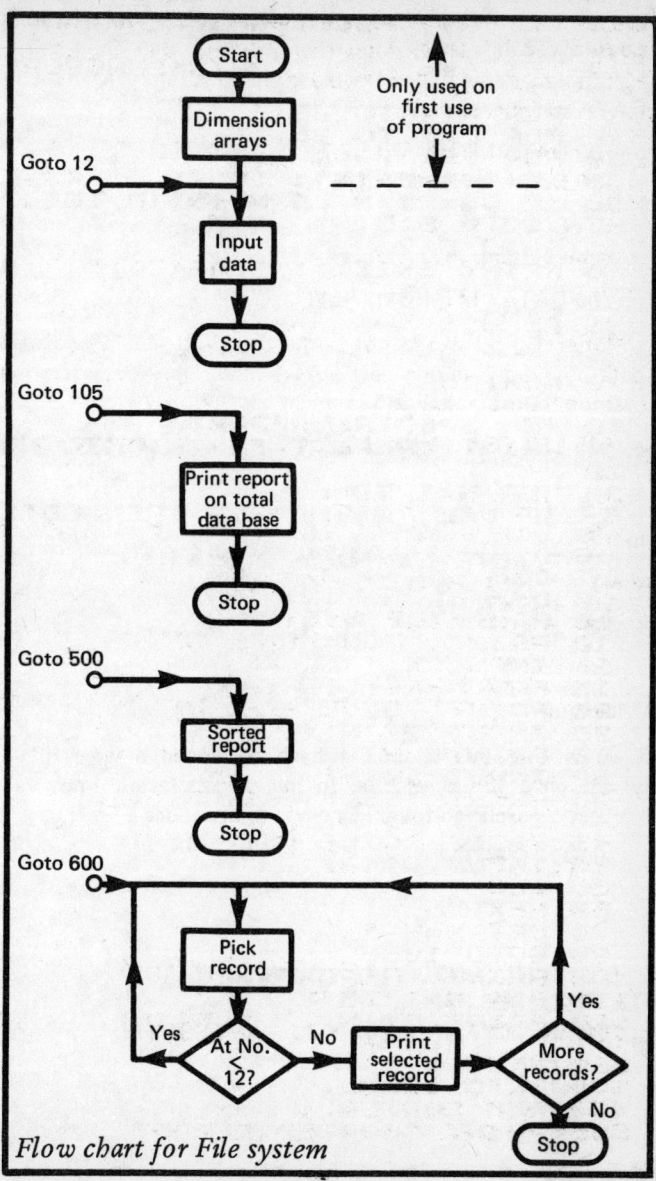

Flow chart for File system

```
510 LET R$="ABCDEFGHIJKLMNOPQRSTUVWXYZ"
512 LET B$="ABCDEFGHIJKLMNOPQRSTUVWXYZ"
520 FOR N=1 TO 26
525 FOR J=1 TO 26
530 FOR Z=1 TO K
535 LET G$=E$(Z,1 TO 2)
538 IF G$=R$(N TO N)+B$(J TO J) THEN GOTO 545
540 GOTO 547
545 PRINT E$(Z);" ";S$(Z);" ";A$(Z);" ";W$(Z)
547 REM
550 NEXT Z
560 NEXT J
570 NEXT N
580 GOTO 1000
600 REM SPECIAL REPORT
610 PRINT "REPORT FOR ATOMIC NO.>12"
630 FOR N=1 TO K
635 IF VAL (A$(N))<12 THEN GOTO 660
650 PRINT E$(N);" ";S$(N);" ";A$(N);" ";W$(N)
660 NEXT N
1000 STOP
```

Addendum

Since writing this chapter I have developed a large filing system on a 48K *Spectrum*. In the process several improvements have occurred to me. One was to introduce a "menu":

```
10 GO TO 800
 .
 .
 .
800 PRINT "ENTER 1 IF YOU WISH TO ADD
   RECORDS:"
820 PRINT "ENTER 2 IF YOU WANT SORTED
   REPORT :'
 .
 .
 .
```

```
850 INPUT C9
860 IF C9=1 THEN GOTO 12
870 IF C9=2 THEN GOTO 500
 .
 .
 .
```

A good plan would be to return always to the menu after each activity using GOTO 800.

To exit from the menu add a conditional jump say IF C9=9 THEN GOTO 1000.

On *Spectrum* use:

SAVE "FILES" LINE 800

This will save your program and data arrays and will auto start at the menu. (Remember to get LINE press CAPS SHIFT and SYMBOL SHIFT to get E prompt then press SYMBOL SHIFT and 3 key.)

Italian

This program is similar in concept to the program Files. On the first run you answer 1 to the intial prompt and start to build your vocabulary data base. Italian words are stored in I$(N), pronunciation in P$(N) and the English equivalents in E$(N).

Suppose you enter 10 for the number of new words to be added. The computer will then prompt you 10 times for each set of data. Thus:

RUN
DO YOU WANT TO 1=ADD NEW VOCAB, 2=TEST
  ITALIAN–ENGLISH, 3=TEST ENGLISH–ITALIAN?
<u>1</u>
HOW MANY WORDS TO ADD?
<u>10</u>
ENTER ITALIAN WORD:
<u>DUCE</u>
ENTER PRONUNCIATION:
<u>DOOCHAY</u>

ENTER ENGLISH WORD:
CHIEF
.
.
.
.
.

After adding the new words the program stops. You can now SAVE the program and its variables and arrays. The number of records in your data base is stored in the variable K.

Now LOAD this program. *Do not use* RUN. Instead use GOTO 45. To add more records answer 1 to the prompt and these new records will automatically be added to the old ones. To test yourself in the language just enter 2 or 3 at the prompt. Always use GOTO 45 to start otherwise you will wipe away your stored data.

I haven't used the pronunciation (stored in P$(N)). However, I thought it might be useful — you could print it back at say line 335.

ZX81 users should enter CONT if they run out of screen. Non *ZX81* users should leave out line 165 which clears the screen.

As it stands the program will store 100 records — see dimension statements. You could keep several copies of the program on tape with different words stored in each.

Lines 320 and 520 assign random numbers between 1 and K (i.e. the number of records) to variable A. On some systems this might become

320 LET A= INT((K*RND(1))+1)

Lines 345 and 545 had to be introduced because in Sinclair BASIC having defined the fields as being 12 characters long M$ can't equal them unless M$ has 12 characters. In line 345 if M$ is less than 12 characters long it is made up to the required 12 characters by adding the correct number of blank spaces. O$ contains these extra spaces which are concatenated (or linked) to M$.

Another feature of this sort of system is that you can

change items in your data easily. For instance if your third record had E$= "CATE" instead of the correct "CAT" you would change it by merely entering

LET E$(3) = "CAT"

This line is entered at system level or at the computer prompt — K on the *ZX81* or *Spectrum*. Having made the change you SAVE it when you have finished using the program.

Again users who haven't got the facility of saving variables can put their data into DATA lines thus:

1000 DATA DUCE, DOOCHAY, CHIEF

They would READ the data into I$(N), P$(N), E$(N) at the start of the program before proceeding to the word tests. New data would be added by simply adding new DATA lines. In this case the objections to RUN don't apply and you must RUN the program to fill the arrays holding the data.

```
   1 REM PROG TO LEARN ITALIAN W
ORDS...
   5 LET K=0
  10 DIM I$(100,12)
  15 DIM P$(100,12)
  20 DIM E$(100,12)
  45 PRINT "DO YOU WANT TO 1=ADD
 NEW VOCAB,2=TEST ITALIAN-ENGLIS
H,3=ENGLISH-ITALIAN?"
  48 INPUT Z
  50 IF Z=1 THEN GOTO 100
  80 IF Z=2 THEN GOTO 300
  90 GOTO 500
 100 PRINT "HOW MANY WORDS TO AD
D?"
 110 INPUT J
 120 FOR N=K+1 TO K+J
 130 PRINT "ENTER ITALIAN WORD:"
 140 INPUT I$(N)
 145 PRINT "ENTER PRONOUNCIATION
:"
 148 INPUT P$(N)
 150 PRINT "ENTER ENGLISH WORD:"
 160 INPUT E$(N)
 165 CLS
```

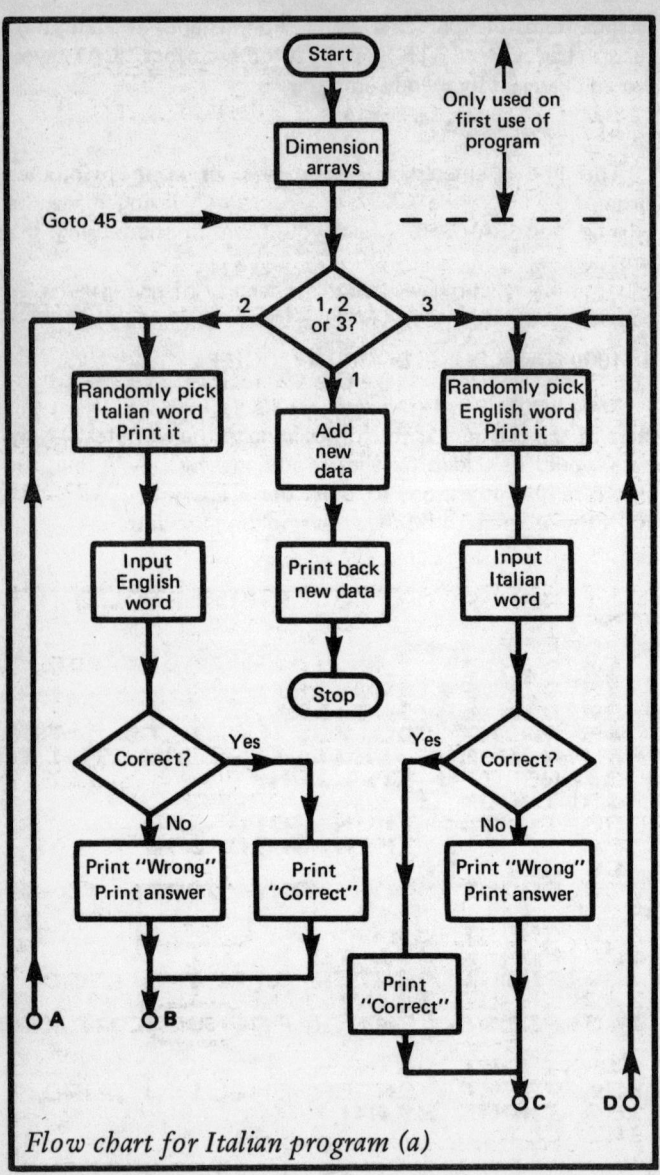

Flow chart for Italian program (a)

```
168 LET K=K+1
170 NEXT N
172 PRINT "NEW VOCAB ADDED:"
175 FOR H=(K-J)+1 TO K
180 PRINT E$(H);I$(H);P$(H)
190 NEXT H
195 GOTO 9999
300 REM TEST ITALIAN-ENGLISH
305 LET Y=0
308 LET O$="                "
310 FOR N=1 TO 10
320 LET A=INT ((RND*K)+1)
325 LET H$=E$(A)
330 PRINT "GIVE ENGLISH EQUIVALENT OF ";I$(A)
340 INPUT M$
345 LET M$=M$+O$(((LEN M$)+1) TO 12)
350 IF M$=H$ THEN LET Y=Y+1
360 IF M$=H$ THEN PRINT "CORRECT."
370 IF M$<>H$ THEN PRINT "WRONG ANSWER = ";H$
```

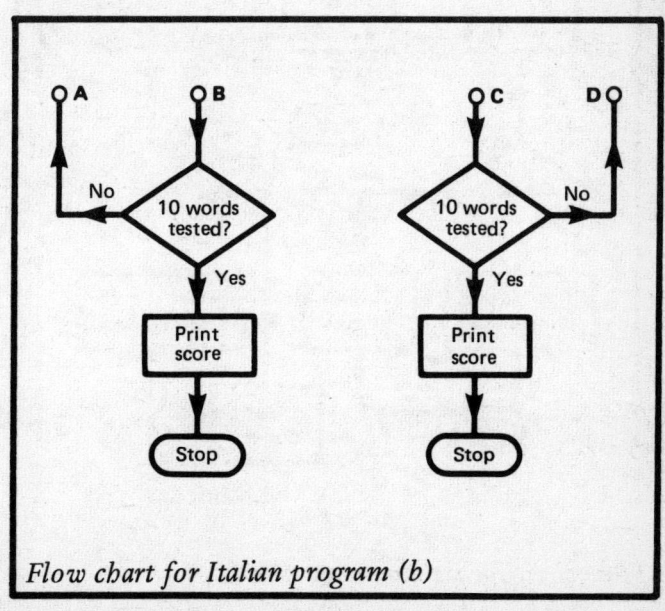

Flow chart for Italian program (b)

```
380 NEXT N
390 PRINT "SCORE=";Y;" OUT OF 10"
400 GOTO 9999
500 REM TEST ENGLISH-ITALIAN
505 LET Y=0
510 LET O$="            "
515 FOR N=1 TO 10
520 LET A=INT ((RND*K)+1)
525 LET H$=I$(A)
530 PRINT "GIVE ITALIAN EQUIVALENT OF ";E$(A)
540 INPUT M$
545 LET M$=M$+O$(((LEN M$)+1) TO 12)
550 IF M$=H$ THEN LET Y=Y+1
560 IF M$=H$ THEN PRINT "CORRECT."
570 IF M$<>H$ THEN PRINT "WRONG ANSWER = ";H$
580 NEXT N
590 PRINT "SCORE=";Y;" OUT OF 10"
600 GOTO 9999
9999 STOP
```

(N.B. Spectrum users do not forget to:
SAVE "ITALIAN" LINE 45)

Chapter 6

ENGINEERING APPLICATIONS

(Note *Spectrum* and some other systems use up arrow ↑ instead of ** for raising a variable to a power.)

Complex Numbers — the j Operator

At one time I had a lot of work to do involving complex numbers. I therefore developed a computer routine to add, subtract, multiply and divide two such numbers.

Initially I wrote a program that for multiplication and division followed the logical long hand method of converting the a+jb format into the polar form $A\angle\theta$. To my consternation on checking out the program it sometimes gave the wrong answer.

Eventually I discovered that there was nothing wrong with the algorithm which exactly followed the way you would do it with pen and paper. The problem lay with the function ATN. This is the arctan sometimes written $\tan^{-1}$; so that arctan X means the angle whose tangent is X.

Now my home computer manual gave no limitations on the use of this function. However, seeing nothing wrong logically I checked the function on my machine with the following routine

```
5 FOR N = 1 TO 360
10 REM CONV FROM DEGREES TO RADIANS :
20 LET Y = N*(PI/180)
30 LET Z = TAN(Y)
40 LET C = ATN(Z)
50 PRINT "ANGLE=";N;" CALC ANGLE=";C*180/PI
60 NEXT N
9999 STOP
```
(Note PI = π = 3.142; On some systems : 9999 END)

This proved that ATN didn't always work. I then checked in a manual of a mainframe computer. This machine didn't

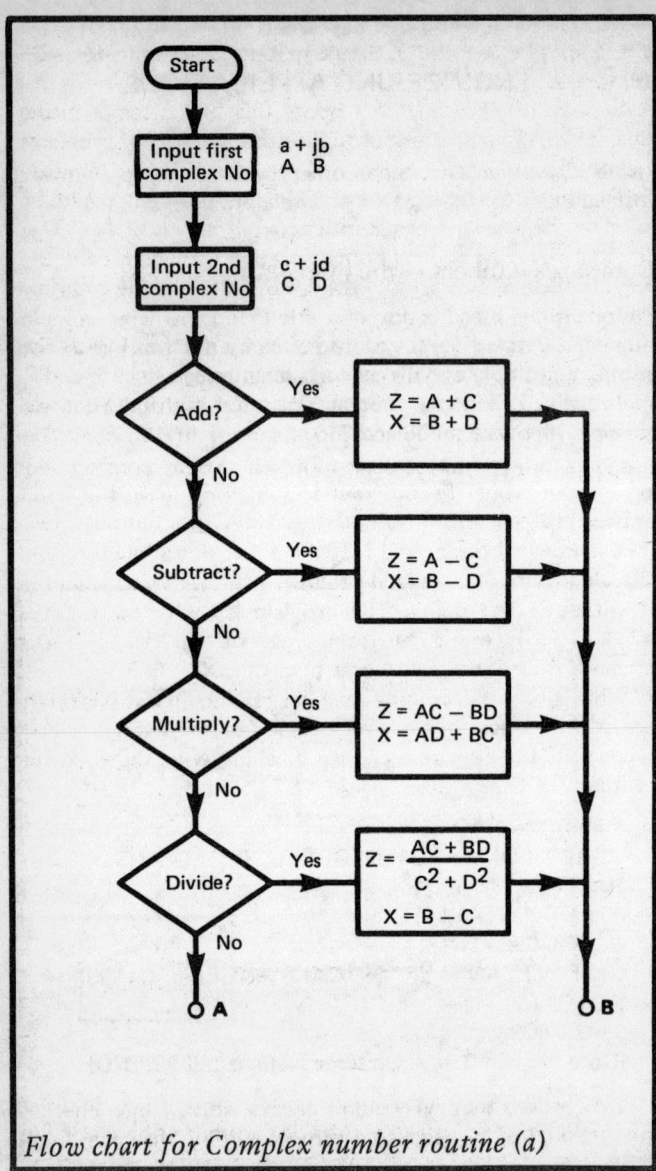

Flow chart for Complex number routine (a)

have the function ATN but for ASN it quoted limits of $-\pi/2$ to $\pi/2$ (or $-90°$ to $+90°$). Similarly it imposed limits for ACS of 0 to π ($0°$ to $180°$).

Anyway for information I quote this first attempt in the appendix. I thought it useful to illustrate the sort of problems that can occur even if you are well versed in BASIC. Of course within the limits imposed by ATN this program could be useful to change a+jb format into polar.

Finally I fell back on algebraic notation throughout and the program seemed to work perfectly. I think the listing and flow chart are self explanatory.

One afterthought — if you don't input a number 1–4 at the prompt you will probably get an error message since Z and X aren't defined. To make routine fool proof in this respect add 2 extra lines between 200 and 210 :

PRINT "ERROR" : GOTO 9999

This program adds, subtracts, divides or multiplies two

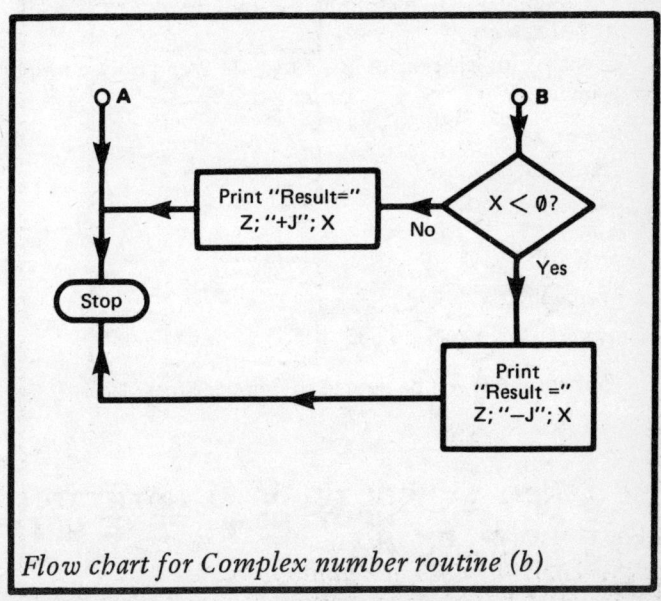

Flow chart for Complex number routine (b)

complex numbers. On running the program you are prompted for the first complex number, real part and then the j part. You are then prompted for the second number in the same way. Consider the example of 2 complex numbers : 1+j8 and 3−j6. Your program run would look like this:

RUN
INPUT REAL PART OF FIRST COMPLEX NO. :
<u>1</u>
INPUT UNREAL OR J PART OF THE FIRST
  COMPLEX NO. :
<u>8</u>
INPUT REAL PART OF SECOND COMPLEX NUMBER :
<u>3</u>
INPUT REAL OR J PART OF SECOND COMPLEX NO.
<u>−6</u>
ENTER 1 FOR ADDITION . . . etc
<u>1</u>

The computer should eventually output :
RESULT = 4 +J2
Similarly for division of 8−j4 by −7+j2 and only quoting your inputs.

<u>8</u>
<u>−4</u>
<u>−7</u>
<u>2</u>
<u>4</u>   (for division)

The computer should print back:

RESULT = −1.208 + J.226

(Perhaps result will be quoted to more decimal places.)

```
   1 REM SYMBOLIC OR J NOTATION:
  10 PRINT "INPUT REAL PART OF F
IRST COMPLEX NO.:"
  20 INPUT A
```

```
30 PRINT "INPUT UNREAL OR J PART OF FIRST COMPLEX NO.:"
40 INPUT B
50 PRINT "INPUT REAL PART OF SECOND COMPLEX NO.:"
60 INPUT C
70 PRINT "INPUT UNREAL OR J PART OF SECOND COMPLEX NO.:"
80 INPUT D
100 REM MENU...
110 PRINT "ENTER 1 FOR ADDITION"
120 PRINT "2 FOR SUBTRACTION"
130 PRINT "3 FOR MULTIPLICATION"
140 PRINT "OR 4 FOR DIVISION:"
150 INPUT V
160 IF V=1 THEN GOSUB 500
170 IF V=2 THEN GOSUB 600
180 IF V=3 THEN GOSUB 700
190 IF V=4 THEN GOSUB 800
200 IF X<0 THEN GOTO 240
210 PRINT "RESULT=";Z;"+J";X
220 GOTO 9999
240 PRINT "RESULT=";Z;"-J";ABS(X)
300 GOTO 9999
500 REM ADD SUBR...
510 LET Z=A+C
520 LET X=B+D
590 RETURN
600 REM SUBTRACTION SUBR...
610 LET Z=A-C
620 LET X=B-D
690 RETURN
700 REM MULTIPLICATION SUBR.
710 LET Z=(A*C)-(B*D)
720 LET X=(A*D)+(B*C)
790 RETURN
800 REM DIVISION SUBR...
810 LET Z=((A*C)+(B*D))/(C*C+D*D)
820 LET X=((B*C)-(A*D))/(C*C+D*D)
890 RETURN
9999 STOP
```

Binary/Hexadecimal/Decimal Conversion Program

This program will convert from anyone of these number systems to any other. Considering the various sections of the program

Binary to Decimal

The binary number is input to S$ as a character string. The number of characters in S$ is assigned to L. Each element of S$ is then converted into a number and multiplied by the appropriate power of 2. The resultant values are each stored in the array B(N).

The elements of the array B(N) are then added to give the required decimal value.

Decimal to Binary

The decimal value is assigned to D. S$ is a string initially equal to 23 zeros. The largest value of 2^N is then found where N is an integer and 2^N is just larger than D. The appropriate 0 in S$ is then changed to a 1. This process is reiterated each time subtracting 2^{N-1} from D until D=0 when S$ is printed out as the result.

Binary to Hexadecimal

The binary number is fed in groups of 4 bits at a time. Note the grouping is done from the right but the most significant part is entered first so 1 1 0 1 1 1 1 would be entered:

1 1 0
1 1 1 1

As the binary 4 bit numbers are entered they are assigned to the array B(N). A subroutine converts the binary numbers into hexadecimal equivalents stored in the character array H$(N).

The elements of H$(N) are then added together or more

properly concatenated and the resultant assigned to S$ which
is then printed out as the result.

Hexadecimal to Binary

The hexadecimal number is fed in one character at a time into
the character array H$(N). A subroutine consisting of a look-
up table converts the hex character into the equivalent binary
character. The resultant binary equivalents are stored in B$(N)
another character array. The elements of B$(N) are then con-
catenated together in the string S$ which is eventually printed
out as the answer.

Decimal to Hexadecimal

The decimal number is input to D This time 24 zeros are
assigned to S$ The decimal to binary routine is then used.
(Note in this routine you could use 24 instead of 23 zeros
assigned to S$ but for Dec-Hex we require multiple of 4).

Having got the binary equivalent and assigned it to S$ this is
converted to the hex equivalent. The binary number is
broken down into 4 bit words. These are converted into
numbers by VAL and each number is stored in the array B(N).
The subroutine starting at 830 converts each of these numbers
into the corresponding hex number which is stored in the
character array H$(N).

Each element of H$(N) is then concatenated to G$ and the
resultant value of G$ printed out as the required hexadecimal
value.

Hexadecimal to Decimal

The hex number is fed in one digit at a time and stored in the
character array H$(N). The subroutine starting at line 1110
converts each element of H$(N) to its binary equivalent which
is then stored in character array B$(N). The elements of
B$(N) are then concatenated to the string S$. The routine for
Bin-Dec is then used to convert S$ to a binary number as
previously described.

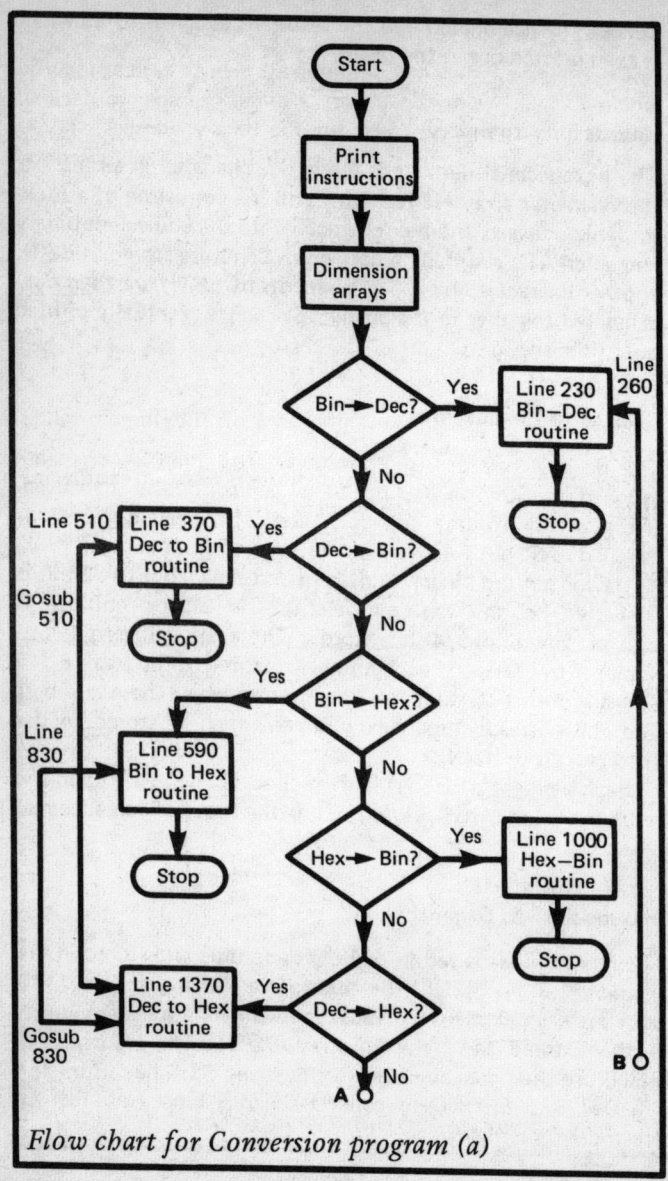

Flow chart for Conversion program (a)

Running Instructions:

On entering RUN the computer asks which conversion you require. If you want to convert a binary number to decimal enter 1. You are then asked for the binary number. If you enter say 1101 the computer after a slight delay will return.

THE DECIMAL NUMBER IS : 13

Try these equivalents to further check this feature

BINARY NUMBER	DECIMAL EQUIVALENT
11101111	239
11010	26
111111	63

Hopefully you got the correct answer on entering the values in the left hand column above.

Now to use the second part of the program. After entering RUN answer the computer's query with a 2. The computer then prompts for a decimal value. If you enter 13 the computer should return 1101. There will be a string of leading zeros but this is just the way the program is written. Similarly

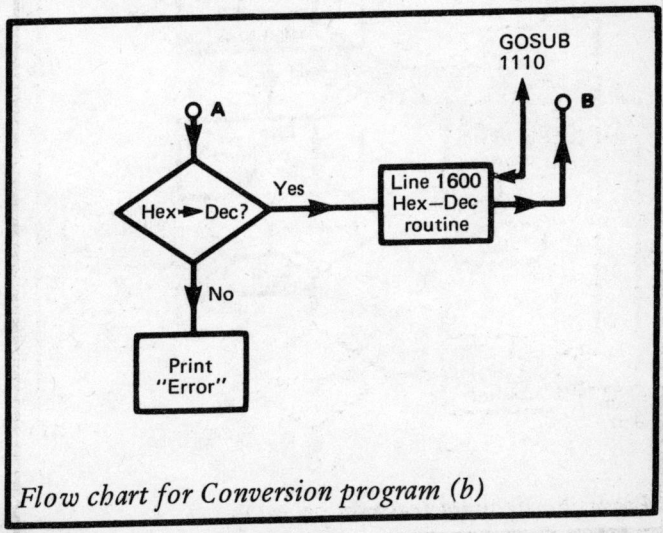

Flow chart for Conversion program (b)

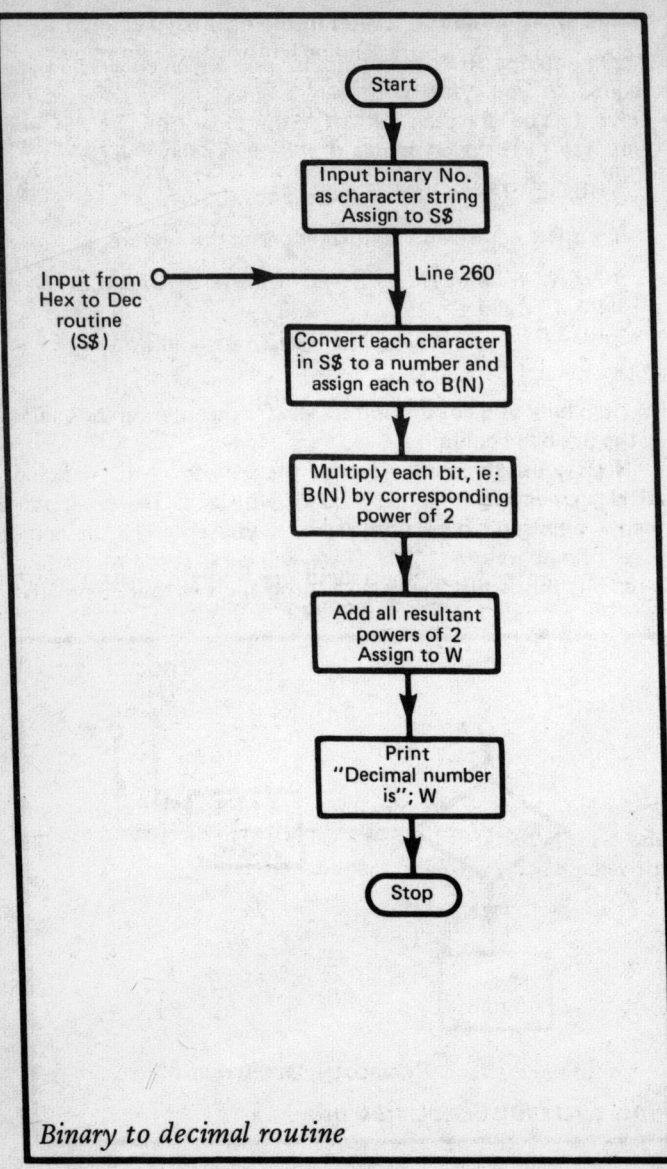

Binary to decimal routine

if you enter any of the values in the right hand column above you should get the corresponding left hand column value.

To convert binary numbers to hexadecimal enter 3 at the initial prompt. The way the program is written requires that you divide your binary number into groups of 4 bits starting from the right and enter the most significant groups first. For example 1 1 1 0 1 1 1 1 would be entered thus

1 1 1 0
1 1 1 1
9

The 9 ends your input. The computer should return EF as the required hex number.

Again giving you some trial material:

BINARY	HEX
1 1 1 1 1 1 1 1	FF
1 1 0 0 1 0 0 0	C8
1 1 1 1 1 0 0 0 0 0 1 0 1 1 0 0	F82C

To ensure that you understand the system the last of these Bin/Hex conversions would require the following entries

1 1 1 1
1 0 0 0
0 0 1 0
1 1 0 0
9

On entering 4 at the initial prompt for Hex/Bin conversion you are requested for the hex value a digit at a time. Taking the value F82C you would therefore enter:

F
8
2
C
X

X ends the input. The computer should return:

1 1 1 1 1 0 0 0 0 0 1 0 1 1 0 0

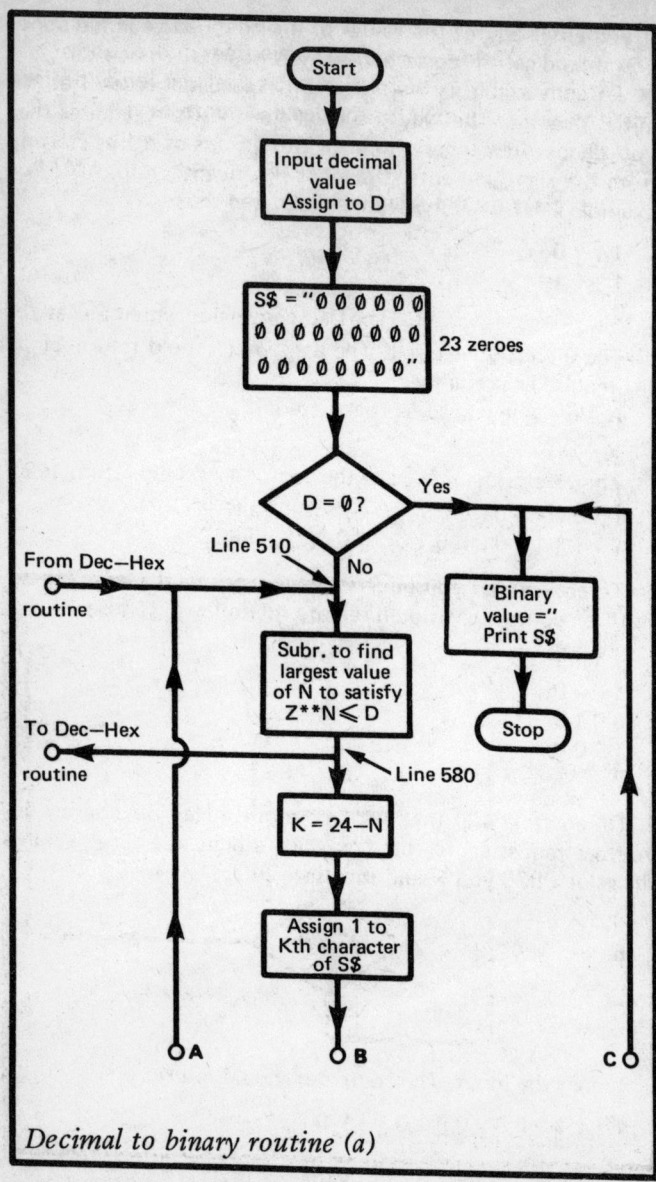

Decimal to binary routine (a)

Similarly as a check that you have entered the program correctly try the other Hex/Bin conversions quoted above.

To do a Dec/Hex conversion enter 5 at the initial prompt. You are then requested for the decimal number e.g.

192

The computer should now return

: 0 0 0 0 C 0

Ignore the colon and leading zeros.

Finally to achieve a Hex/Dec conversion enter a 6 at the start prompt. Then:

C
0
X

The X ends the input and the computer should return 192. Here are some more Hex/Dec equivalents to try

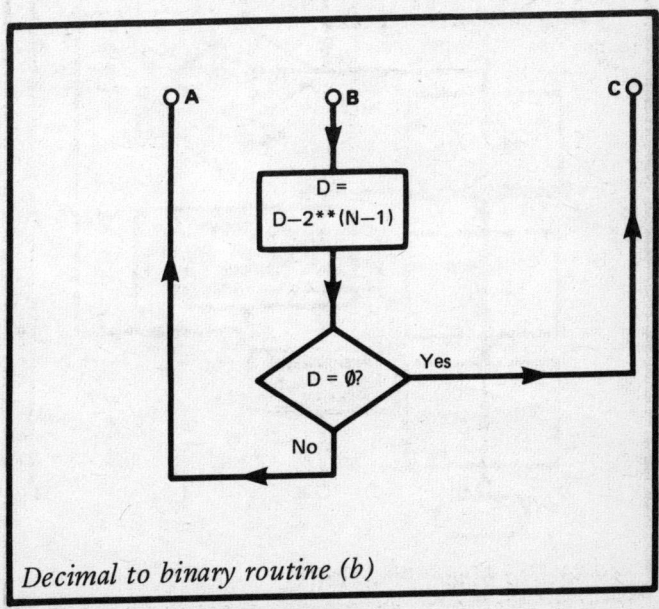

Decimal to binary routine (b)

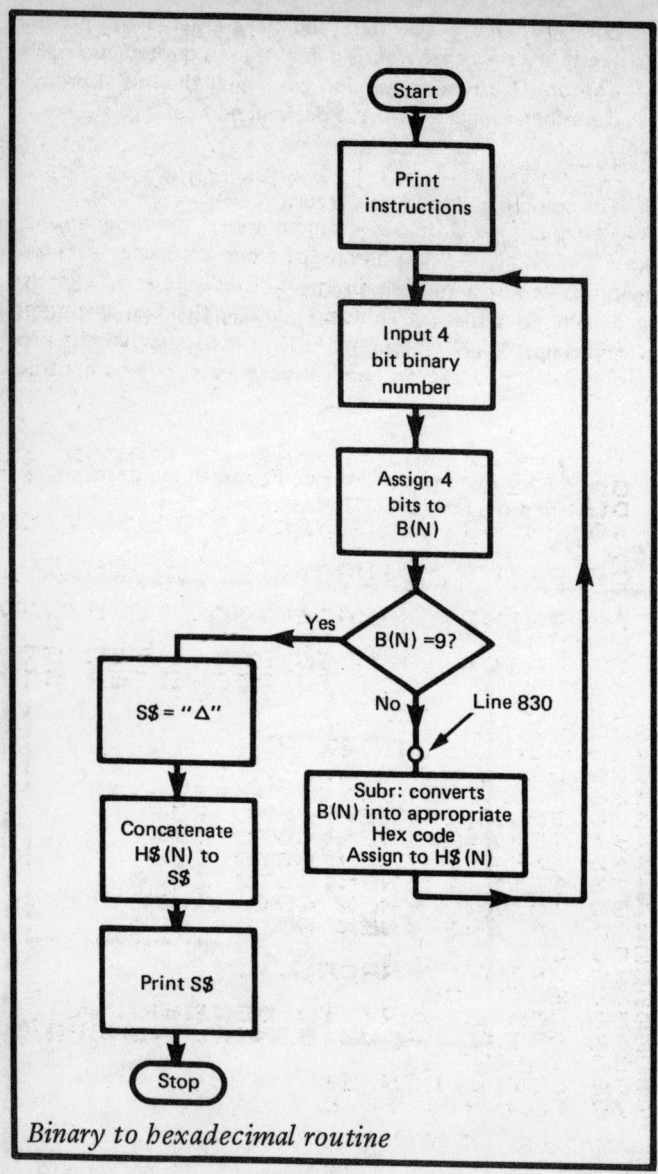

Binary to hexadecimal routine

DECIMAL	HEXADECIMAL
243	F3
255	FF
175	AF
63532	F82C
114688	1C000

WARNING: If you use very large numbers the program may break down due to limitations of your computer or more likely limits built into the program. I leave it as an exercise for you to work out the limits on numbers that can be entered at each phase of the program. Suffice it to say that the program is applicable to most applications met with in computing.

```
1 REM BIN/HEX/DEC COVERTOR...
30 PRINT "IF YOU WANT BINARY TO DECIMAL    ENTER 1"
40 PRINT "DECIMAL TO BINARY ENTER 2"
50 PRINT "BINARY TO HEX ENTER 3"
60 PRINT "HEXADECIMAL TO BINARY ENTER 4"
70 PRINT "DEC TO HEX ENTER 5"
80 PRINT "HEX TO DEC ENTER 6"
90 INPUT X
100 DIM B(48)
110 DIM B$(48,4)
120 DIM H$(48,1)
130 PRINT "****************"
140 IF X=1 THEN GOTO 230
150 IF X=2 THEN GOTO 370
160 IF X=3 THEN GOTO 590
170 IF X=4 THEN GOTO 1000
180 IF X=5 THEN GOTO 1370
190 IF X=6 THEN GOTO 1600
200 CLS
210 PRINT "ERROR...."
220 GOTO 30
230 REM BINARY TO DECIMAL...
240 PRINT "GIVE BINARY NUMBER:"
250 INPUT S$
260 LET L=LEN S$
270 FOR N=1 TO L
```

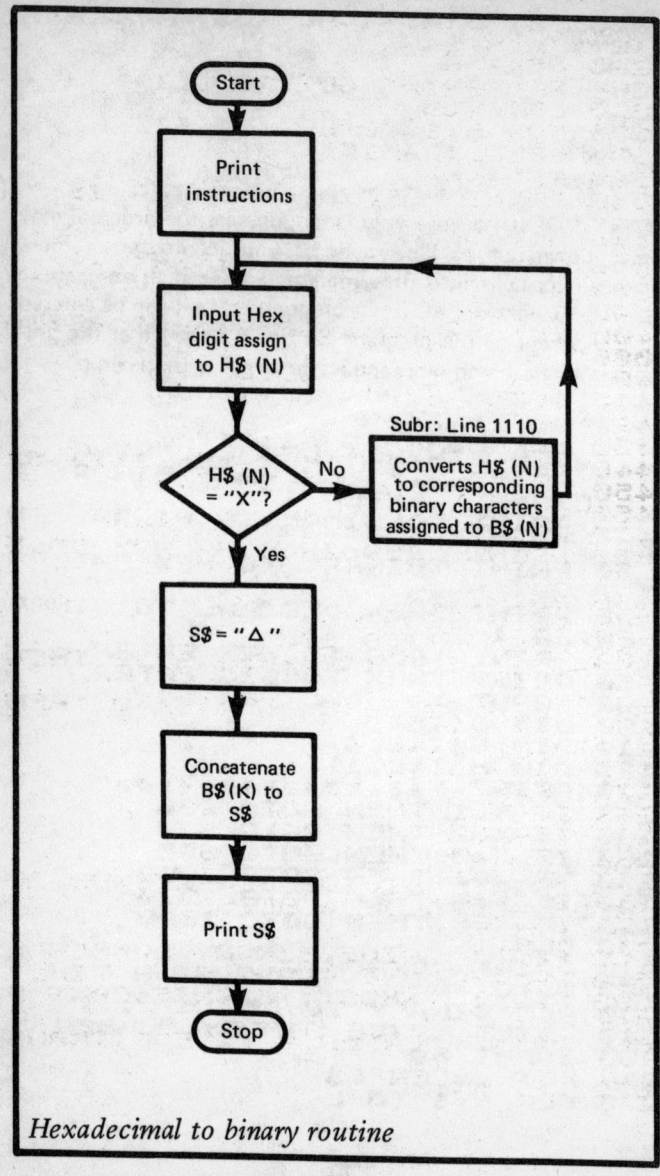

Hexadecimal to binary routine

```
280 LET B(N)=(VAL (S$(N TO N)))
*(2**(L-N))
290 NEXT N
300 REM PRINT OUT RESULT
310 LET W=0
320 FOR K=1 TO L
330 LET W=W+B(K)
340 NEXT K
350 PRINT "DECIMAL NUMBER IS:";
W
360 GOTO 9999
370 REM DECIMAL TO BINARY...
380 PRINT "GIVE DECIMAL VALUE:"
390 INPUT D
400 LET S$="0000000000000000000
0000"
405 IF D=0 THEN GOTO 470
410 GOSUB 510
420 LET K=24-N
430 LET S$(K TO K)="1"
440 LET D=D-INT ((2**(N-1))+.5)
450 IF D=0 THEN GOTO 470
460 GOTO 410
470 PRINT "*****************"
480 PRINT "REQUIRED BINARY VALU
E="
490 PRINT S$
500 GOTO 9999
510 FOR N=1 TO 100
520 IF D-INT ((2**N)+.5)>0 THEN
 GOTO 570
530 IF D-INT ((2**N)+.5)=0 THEN
 GOTO 550
540 GOTO 580
550 LET N=N+1
560 GOTO 580
570 NEXT N
580 RETURN
590 REM BIN TO HEX...
600 PRINT "DIVIDE BINARY NUMBER
 INTO GROUPS OF 4 BITS"
620 LET N=0
630 PRINT "GIVE BINARY NUMBER"
640 PRINT "ONE GROUP AT A TIME"
650 PRINT "*MOST* SIGNIFICANT F
IRST"
660 PRINT "ENTER 9 TO END INPUT
"
670 LET N=N+1
```

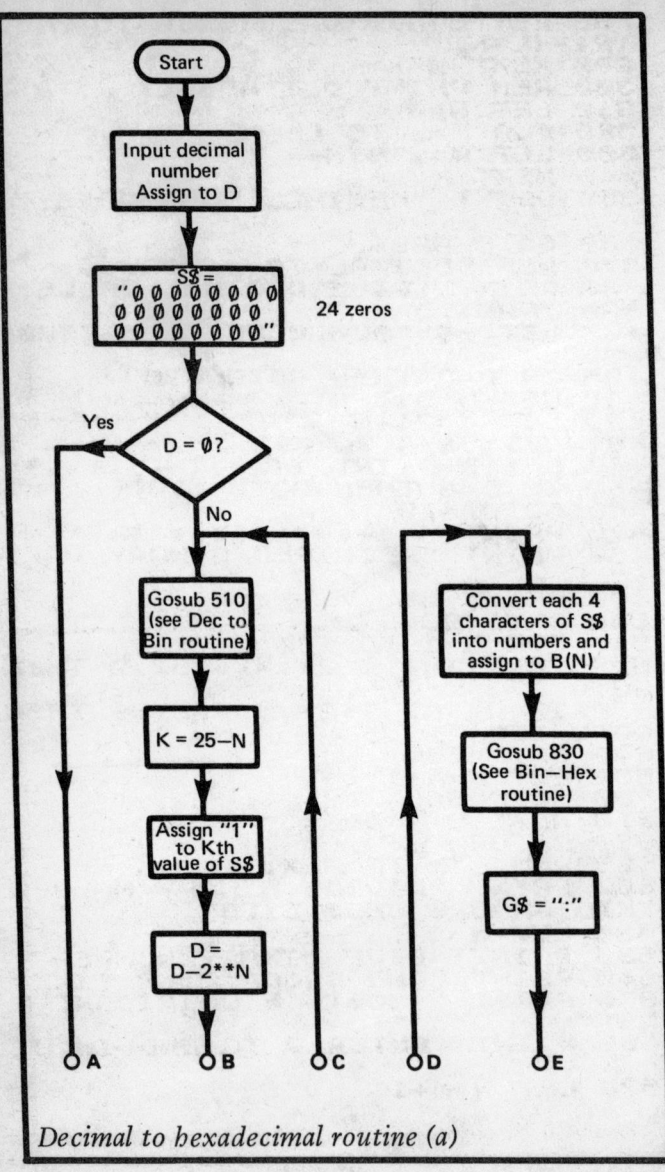

Decimal to hexadecimal routine (a)

```
680 INPUT B(N)
690 IF B(N)=9 THEN GOTO 720
700 GOSUB 830
710 GOTO 670
720 REM PRINT RESULT...
730 PRINT "±±±±±±±±±±±±±±±±"
740 PRINT "RESULT OF CONVERSION"
750 PRINT "±MOST± SIGNIFICANT"
760 PRINT "PART FIRST:"
770 LET S$=" "
780 FOR K=1 TO N
790 LET S$=S$+H$(K)
800 NEXT K
810 PRINT S$
820 GOTO 9999
830 REM SUBR FOR CONVERSION.
835 IF B(N)=0 THEN LET H$(N)="0"
840 IF B(N)=1 THEN LET H$(N)="1"
850 IF B(N)=10 THEN LET H$(N)="2"
860 IF B(N)=11 THEN LET H$(N)="3"
```

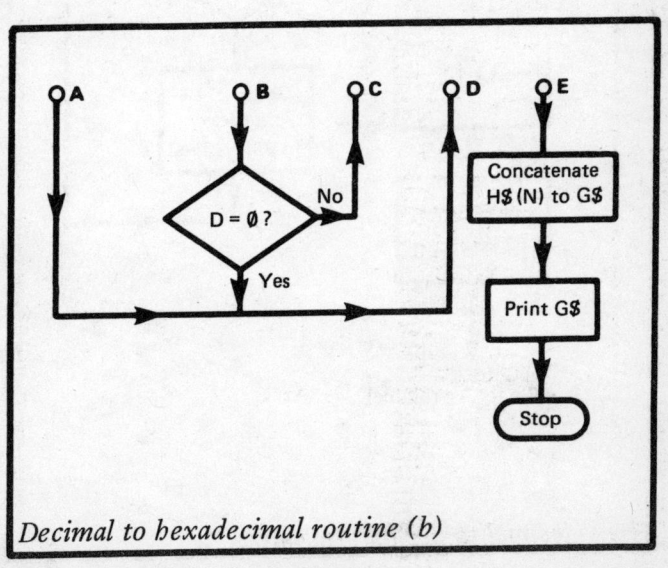

Decimal to hexadecimal routine (b)

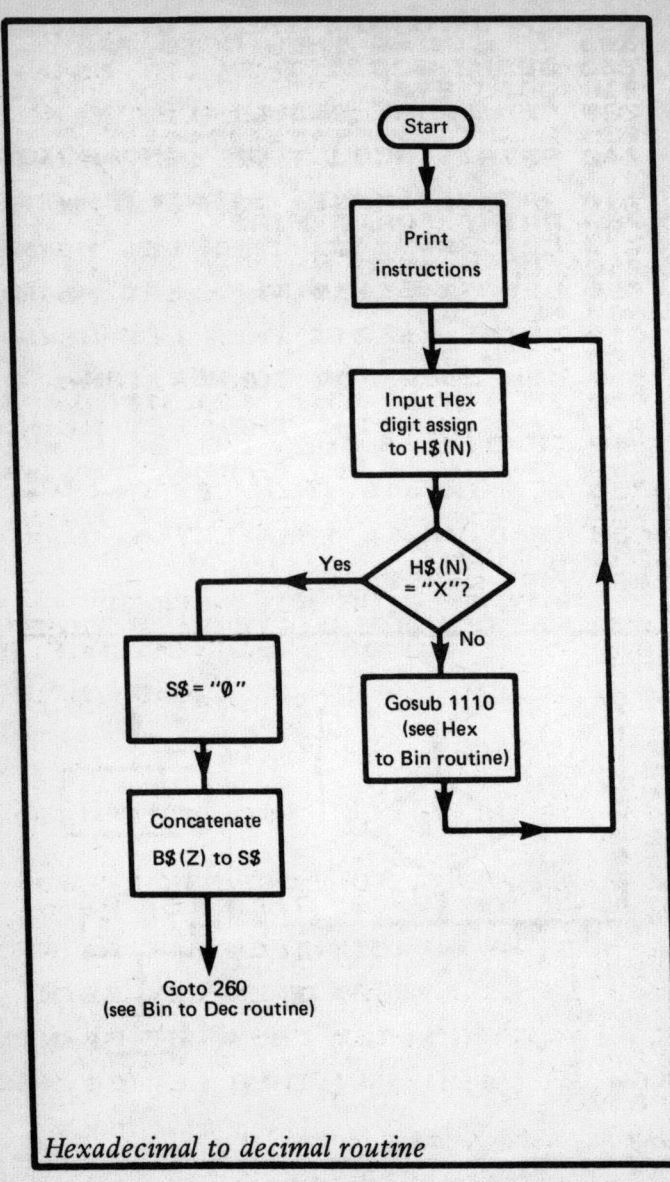

Hexadecimal to decimal routine

```
 870 IF B(N)=100 THEN LET H$(N)=
"4"
 880 IF B(N)=101 THEN LET H$(N)=
"5"
 890 IF B(N)=110 THEN LET H$(N)=
"6"
 900 IF B(N)=111 THEN LET H$(N)=
"7"
 910 IF B(N)=1000 THEN LET H$(N)
="8"
 920 IF B(N)=1001 THEN LET H$(N)
="9"
 930 IF B(N)=1010 THEN LET H$(N)
="A"
 940 IF B(N)=1011 THEN LET H$(N)
="B"
 950 IF B(N)=1100 THEN LET H$(N)
="C"
 960 IF B(N)=1101 THEN LET H$(N)
="D"
 970 IF B(N)=1110 THEN LET H$(N)
="E"
 980 IF B(N)=1111 THEN LET H$(N)
="F"
 990 RETURN
1000 REM HEX TO BINARY...
1010 PRINT "GIVE HEX NUMBER"
1020 PRINT "ONE DIGIT AT A TIME"
1030 PRINT ":MOST: SIGNIFICANT P
ARTS FIRST"
1040 PRINT "ENTER X TO END INPUT
:"
1050 LET N=0
1060 LET N=N+1
1070 INPUT H$(N)
1080 IF H$(N)="X" THEN GOTO 1290
1090 GOSUB 1110
1100 GOTO 1060
1110 REM SUBR TO FIND BIN EQUIV.
1120 IF H$(N)="0" THEN LET B$(N)
="0000"
1130 IF H$(N)="1" THEN LET B$(N)
="0001"
1140 IF H$(N)="2" THEN LET B$(N)
="0010"
1150 IF H$(N)="3" THEN LET B$(N)
="0011"
1160 IF H$(N)="4" THEN LET B$(N)
="0100"
```

```
1170 IF H$(N)="5" THEN LET B$(N)
="0101"
1180 IF H$(N)="6" THEN LET B$(N)
="0110"
1190 IF H$(N)="7" THEN LET B$(N)
="0111"
1200 IF H$(N)="8" THEN LET B$(N)
="1000"
1210 IF H$(N)="9" THEN LET B$(N)
="1001"
1220 IF H$(N)="A" THEN LET B$(N)
="1010"
1230 IF H$(N)="B" THEN LET B$(N)
="1011"
1240 IF H$(N)="C" THEN LET B$(N)
="1100"
1250 IF H$(N)="D" THEN LET B$(N)
="1101"
1260 IF H$(N)="E" THEN LET B$(N)
="1110"
1270 IF H$(N)="F" THEN LET B$(N)
="1111"
1280 RETURN
1290 REM PRINT RESULTS...
1300 LET S$=" "
1310 PRINT "BINARY EQUIV.="
1320 FOR K=1 TO N-1
1330 LET S$=S$+B$(K)
1340 NEXT K
1350 PRINT S$
1360 GOTO 9999
1370 REM DEC TO HEX CONVERSION.
1380 PRINT "GIVE DECIMAL NUMBER:
"
1390 INPUT D
1400 LET S$="000000000000000000000000"
1405 IF D=0 THEN GOTO 1470
1410 GOSUB 510
1420 LET K=25-N
1430 LET S$(K TO K)="1"
1440 LET D=D-INT ((2**(N-1))+.5)
1450 IF D=0 THEN GOTO 1470
1460 GOTO 1410
1470 REM GOT S$ NOW CONV TO HEX.
1480 FOR N=1 TO 21 STEP 4
1490 LET B(N)=VAL (S$(N TO N+3))
1500 GOSUB 830
1510 NEXT N
1520 REM PRINT OUT HEX EQUIV.
```

```
1530 PRINT "HEX. EQUIV.="
1540 LET G$=":"
1550 FOR N=1 TO 21 STEP 4
1560 LET G$=G$+H$(N)
1570 NEXT N
1580 PRINT G$
1590 GOTO 9999
1600 REM HEX TO DEC SUBR.
1610 PRINT "GIVE HEX NUMBER"
1620 PRINT "ONE DIGIT AT A TIME"
1630 PRINT "*MOST* SIGNIFICANT PARTS FIRST"
1640 PRINT "ENTER X TO END INPUT."
1650 LET N=0
1660 LET N=N+1
1670 INPUT H$(N)
1680 IF H$(N)="X" THEN GOTO 1710
1690 GOSUB 1110
1700 GOTO 1660
1710 REM TO LINK BIN. NOS.
1720 LET S$="0"
1730 FOR Z=1 TO N-1
1740 LET S$=S$+B$(Z)
1750 NEXT Z
1760 GOTO 260
9999 STOP
```

Superhet

To cover the broadest spectrum of applications I decided to include a typical servicing aid program. These are being found more and more useful in technical applications. In some cases the algorithm is actually programmed into a machine console and helps take the service engineer step by step through the servicing procedure. Very sophisticated systems can also indicate the area where the fault is located.

Obviously in the limited space available I have only room to cover a simple case. Here we are considering a typical transistor MW/LW superhet radio operating from its own batteries or from its own power supply.

On showing the flow chart to a couple of radio enthusiasts one said that it was OK but he preferred working from the symptoms. The other said yes that's the way he tackles fault finding. Again it's a matter of personal choice. You could construct a flow chart centred on symptoms such as "Is there a ponk in the speaker at switch on?" or "Is there a motor-boating effect?" However, this approach would make the program very verbose. Anyway once you have grasped the methodology it should be a straight forward job to write your own program in the way you prefer.

I haven't put any CLS statements in for *ZX81* users so they will have to use CONT when the screen becomes full. My reason for this is that the whole print-out is useful.

As usual non-Sinclair users should use 9999 END and not STOP as shown. Since there is so much text you will probably **require 16K of RAM to load** this program.

```
1 REM SUPERHET SERVICING PROG
10 PRINT "CHECK POWER SUPPLY ON LOAD"
20 PRINT "WITH A MULTIMETER (AT LEAST 20K OHMS/VOLT)"
30 PRINT "IS POWER SUPPLY OK?ANS Y OR N:"
40 INPUT A$
50 IF A$="Y" THEN GOTO 200
60 PRINT "POWER SUPPLY/BATTERY CHK."
70 PRINT "IF PS OK AND BATTERY SUSPECT"
80 PRINT "CHECK BATTERY,BATTERY CONNECTORS"
90 PRINT "AND LEADS, FUSES(IF ANY), ON/OFF"
100 PRINT "SWITCH.IF PS SUSPECT CHK FUSES,"
110 PRINT "ON/OFF SWITCH, REGULATOR TRAN-"
120 PRINT "SISTORS,CHOKES,RECTIFIERS,"
130 GOSUB 3000
150 GOTO 5000
200 PRINT "CHECK AUDIO STAGES WITH AUDIO"
210 PRINT "FREQUENCY SIGNAL GENERATOR."
220 PRINT "IS AF SYSTEM OK?ANS Y OR N:"
230 INPUT A$
240 IF A$="Y" THEN GOTO 600
```

```
250 PRINT "IS THE OUTPUT STAGE OK?ANS Y OR N:"
260 INPUT A$
270 IF A$="Y" THEN GOTO 400
280 PRINT "CHECK LOUDSPEAKER AND ITS LEADS,"
290 PRINT "OUTPUT TRANSFORMER, OUTPUT "
300 PRINT "TRANSISTORS,OUTPUT CIRCUITRY,"
310 GOSUB 3000
330 GOTO 5000
400 PRINT "CHECK  AF STAGES ESPECIALLY COUPLING"
410 PRINT "CAPACITORS,AF TRANSISTORS,"
420 GOSUB 3000
430 GOTO 5000
600 PRINT "CHECK DETECTOR STAGE WITH RF"
610 PRINT "SIGNAL GENERATOR AND SCOPE."
620 PRINT "IS DETECTOR STAGE OK?ANS Y OR N:"
630 INPUT A$
640 IF A$="Y" THEN GOTO 1000
650 PRINT "IS COUPLING TO AF STAGES OK?ANS Y OR N:"
660 INPUT A$
670 IF A$="Y" THEN GOTO 600
680 PRINT "CHECK DETECTOR-AF STAGES"
690 PRINT "COUPLING CIRCUITS."
700 GOSUB 3000
710 GOTO 5000
1000 PRINT "IS AGC WORKING?ANS Y OR N:"
1010 INPUT A$
1020 IF A$="Y" THEN GOTO 1200
1030 PRINT "CHECK AGC DIODE AND"
1040 PRINT "ASSOCIATED CIRCUITRY."
1050 GOSUB 3000
1060 GOTO 5000
1200 PRINT "CHECK INTERMEDIATE FREQUENCY STAGES"
1210 PRINT "USING RADIO FREQUENCY GENERATOR"
1220 PRINT "AND OSCILLOSCOPE."
1230 PRINT "ARE IFS OK?ANS Y OR N:"
```

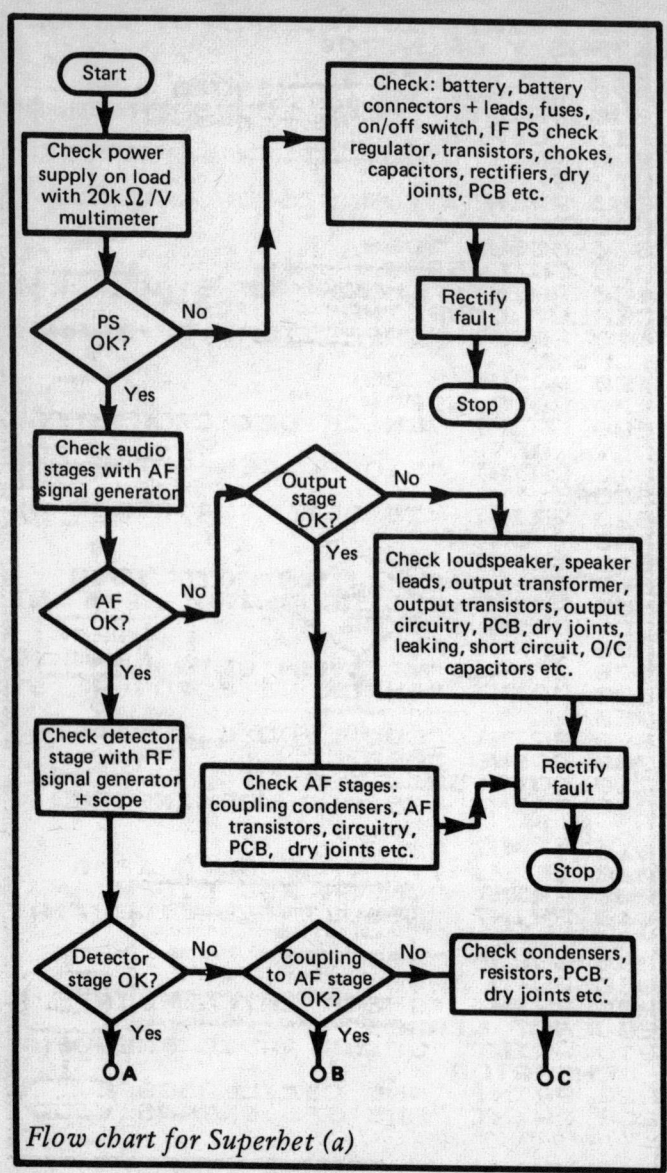

Flow chart for Superhet (a)

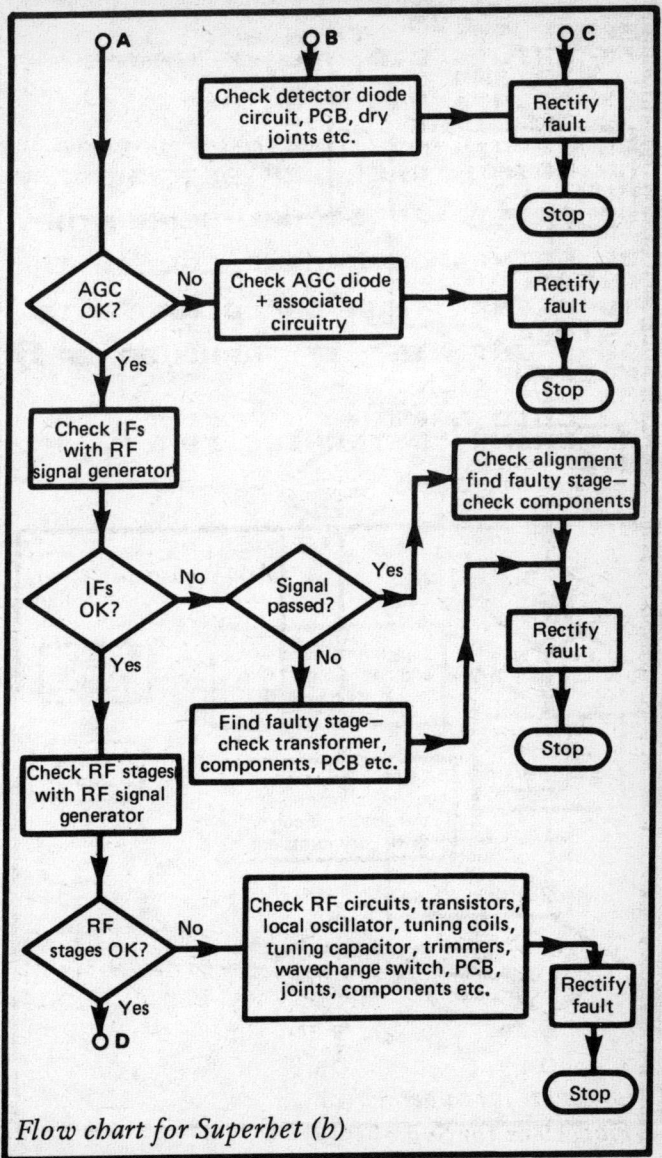

Flow chart for Superhet (b)

```
1240 INPUT A$
1250 IF A$="Y" THEN GOTO 1600
1260 PRINT "DID ALL IF STAGES PASS IF SIGNAL?"
1265 PRINT "ANS Y OR N:"
1270 INPUT A$
1275 IF A$="N" THEN GO TO 1400
1280 PRINT "CHECK IF ALIGNMENT WITH"
1290 PRINT "RF SIGNAL GENERATOR."
1300 PRINT "DETERMINE FAULTY IF STAGE"
1310 PRINT "THEN CHK COMPONENTS IN STAGE,"
1320 PRINT "IE. IF TRANSFORMER,TRANSISTOR."
1330 GOSUB 3000
1340 GOTO 5000
1400 PRINT "DETERMINE FAULTY IF STAGE"
```

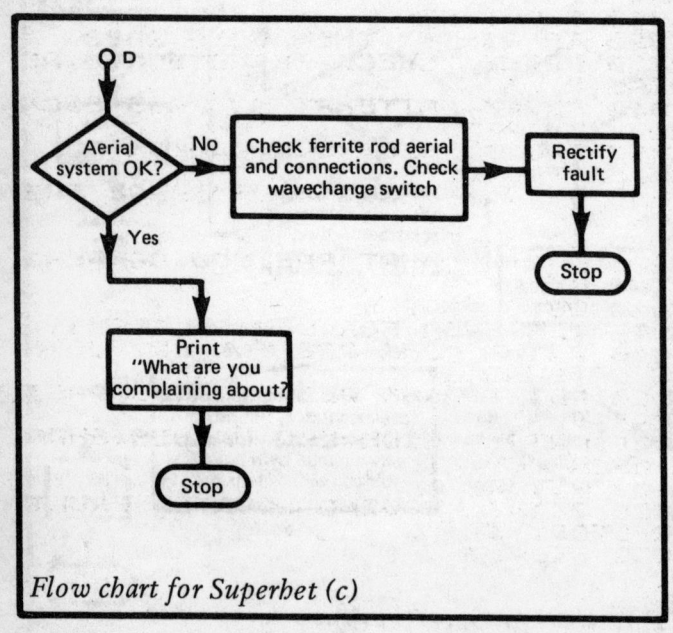

Flow chart for Superhet (c)

```
1410 PRINT "THEN CHK COMPONENTS IN THIS STAGE,"
1420 PRINT "IE. IF TRANSFORMER,TRANSISTOR,"
1430 GOSUB 3000
1440 GOTO 5000
1600 PRINT "CHECK RF STAGES WITH RF"
1610 PRINT "SIGNAL GENERATOR."
1620 PRINT "ARE RF STAGES OK?ANS Y OR N:"
1630 INPUT A$
1640 IF A$="Y" THEN GOTO 1800
1650 PRINT "CHECK RF CIRCUITS-TRANSISTORS,"
1660 PRINT "TUNING CAPACITOR AND TRIMMERS,LOCAL OSCILLATOR,"
1670 PRINT "TUNING COILS,WAVECHANGE SWITCH,"
1680 GOSUB 3000
1690 GOTO 5000
1800 PRINT "IS AERIAL SYSTEM OK? ANS Y OR N:"
1810 INPUT A$
1820 IF A$="Y" THEN GOTO 2000
1830 PRINT "CHECK FERRITE ROD AERIAL."
1840 PRINT "ATTEMPT TO PASS SIGNAL WITH RF"
1850 PRINT "SIG. GEN. CHECK ALL CONNECTIONS."
1860 PRINT "CHECK WAVECHANGE SWITCH."
1870 GOTO 5000
2000 PRINT "WHAT ARE YOU COMPLAINING ABOUT?"
2010 GOTO 9999
3000 REM SUBR FOR COMMON ITEMS..
3010 PRINT "CHK PCB FOR DRY JOINTS OR CRACKS"
3020 PRINT "CHK RESISTORS/CAPACITORS FOR: "
3030 PRINT "HIGH/LOW VALUES,SHORT/OPEN CCT."
3100 RETURN
5000 PRINT "HAVING LOCATED FAULT RECTIFY IT."
9999 STOP
```

Chapter 7

STATISTICS

In preparing this section I have omitted the usual stats programs because they are adequately covered elsewhere in "Babani" books. Instead I quote several programs that I have found useful in engineering and gambling applications. Since space is limited I can't explain the statistical terms used in any detail but you should find them explained in most textbooks on statistics.

Binomial

In a situation where there is a distinct probability of success or failure we can use this program which is based on the binomial distribution. I think it is easier to explain by quoting a typical run:

<u>RUN</u>
GIVE PROBABILITY OF EVENT :
<u>.1</u>
GIVE NO. OF INDEPENDENT TRIALS :
<u>12</u>
GIVE NO. OF EVENTS TO OCCUR IN 12 TRIALS:
MINIMUM :
<u>0</u>
MAXIMUM
<u>8</u>
FOR 12 TRIALS

NO.	PROB.
0	28
1	38
2	23
3	9
4	2
5	0
6	0

| 7 | 0 |
| 8 | 0 |

OK what does this mean? Well if the chance of an event occurring such as finding a rotten apple in a load of apples is 10% (or .1) and we choose 12 apples, the chance of having no bad apples in our sample is 28% (or .28). Similarly the chances of having 1 bad apple is 38%, 2 bad apples 23% etc.

If we require to test the hypothesis that 10% of the apples are bad we could design an experiment in which we randomly select 12 apples and test to see how many are rotten. Suppose none are bad. From the above print-out the chance (or probability) of this occurring based on the assumption that 10% of the population are bad is 28%. Conversely we can say that we are (100−28)% or 72% confident that the population from which the apples were drawn has less than 10% bad apples.

We might require more confidence in our test than 72% so imagine we take 20 apples in our sample. With 20 independent trials and zero events (i.e. no bad apples) we get the probability or chance to be 12% Hence we would be (100−12)% or 88% confident that the percentage of bad apples was less than 10%

Consider an application such as coin tossing. In tossing a coin the probability of the result being heads is 50% or .5. Consider 6 trials. The number of possible heads ranges from 0 to 6. Applying the program:

```
RUN
GIVE PROBABILITY OF EVENT :
.5
GIVE NO. OF INDEPENDENT TRIALS:
6
GIVE NO. OF EVENTS TO OCCUR IN 6 TRIALS :
MINIMUM :
0
MAXIMUM :
6
```

FOR 6 TRIALS :
No.	PROB.
0	2
1	9
2	23
3	31
4	23
5	9
6	2

We therefore have a 23% chance of getting 2 heads and 4 tails; a 2% chance of 6 tails etc.

As it stands the program is limited by the arithmetic overflow resulting from using a large number for the number of events and/or trials. The problem arises in the subroutine (line 1000) which calculates S_{C_R}. An amendment that improves matters is:

```
1020 LET Q=0
1030 LET W=0
1065 IF T>10**30 THEN LET Q=Q+1
1067 IF T>10**30 THEN LET T=T/1000
1095 IF D>10**30 THEN LET W=W+1
1097 IF D>10**30 THEN LET D=D/1000
1120 LET G=(T/D)*(1000**(Q-W))
```

This works albeit slowly. I leave you to devise a more elegant solution.

I don't think we require a flow chart to understand this program. Initially you input the basic data as described above. A$ is assigned a number of spaces and is used to control the output columns. For a number of events in range 10–99 A$ gets one less space to keep output nicely in line. The subroutine calculates the number of combinations of S items taken R at a time S_{C_R} which is the required binomial coefficient. Lines 590 and 600 calculate the probability of the given number of events occurring. Line 610 prints the result.

I think this is all standard BASIC found on most machines. *ZX81* users might want to use FAST at say line 490.

```
 500 PRINT "GIVE PROBABILITY OF
EVENT:"
 510 INPUT P
 520 PRINT "GIVE NO. OF INDEPEND
ENT TRIALS:"
 530 INPUT S
 540 PRINT "GIVE NO. OF EVENTS T
O OCCUR IN ";S;" TRIALS:"
 545 PRINT "MINIMUM:"
 550 INPUT V
 552 PRINT "MAXIMUM:"
 553 INPUT X
 555 PRINT "FOR ";S;" TRIALS "
 560 PRINT "NO.     PROB."
 565 LET A$="      "
 570 FOR J=V TO X
 572 IF J>9 THEN LET A$="     "
 575 LET R=J
 580 GOSUB 1000
 590 LET C=G*(P**R)*((1-P)**(S-R))
 600 LET C=INT ((C*100)+.5)
 610 PRINT J;A$;C
 700 NEXT J
 800 GOTO 9999
1000 REM SUBR TO CALC COMB S(C)R
1045 LET T=1
1050 FOR N=S TO (R+1) STEP -1
1060 LET T=T*N
1070 NEXT N
1075 LET D=1
1080 FOR N=1 TO (S-R)
1090 LET D=D*N
1100 NEXT N
1120 LET G=T/D
1200 RETURN
9999 STOP
```

(N.B. Remember ** is equivalent to ↑)

Exponential (Poisson)

This program is based on the Poisson distribution. Again it is best illustrated with an actual example.

Consider 10 electric motors on test for 100 hours and zero failures occur. The required life of the motor is 100 hours. What is our confidence that the failure rate in the motor population will be less than 5%?

MTBF = Mean Time Between Failures = (100/5)×100 = 2000 hours

Total Time Period = Test time in this case = 10 × 100 = 1000 hours

Now running the program:

```
RUN
GIVE MTBF
2000
GIVE LIFE:
1000
GIVE NO. OF FAILURES:
MINIMUM:
0
MAXIMUM:
5
FLRS        PROB
0           61
1           30
2           8
3           1
4           0
5           0
```

Therefore if zero failures occur the confidence we have in meeting the design goal (i.e. of less than 5% failures) is (100—61) or 39%. Obviously the total test time isn't long enough to ensure a high confidence.

This method is applicable to things like lightning strikes or electronic equipment failures where the events are purely random but we can measure the average rate of occurrence over a long test period.

The program is very similar to the last one but this time we are computing the exponential terms to find the probability of 1, 2 etc events (termed failures on print-out). Again only standard BASIC statements have been used.

```
1 REM EXP PROGRAM...
295 PRINT "EXP. PROBABILITIES."
300 LET E=EXP 1
305 PRINT "GIVE MTBF:"
310 INPUT M
320 PRINT "GIVE LIFE:"
330 INPUT L
340 PRINT "GIVE NO. FAILURES:"
350 PRINT "MINIMUM:"
360 INPUT V
370 PRINT "MAXIMUM:"
380 INPUT X
385 LET A$="        "
390 PRINT "FLRS      PROB."
400 FOR J=V TO X
410 LET R=J
415 IF J>9 THEN LET A$="       "
420 GOSUB 2000
430 LET C=INT ((C*100)+.5)
440 PRINT J;A$;C
460 NEXT J
490 GOTO 9999
2000 REM SUBR TO FIND EXP. PROB.
2005 LET D=1
2010 FOR N=1 TO R
2020 LET D=D*N
2030 NEXT N
2100 LET C=(((L/M)**R)/D)*(E**(-L/M))
2500 RETURN
9999 STOP
```

Runs-test

Often we get data from some measurements and we wish to know if it is purely random. Data such as the toss of a coin (heads or tails), the spin of a roulette wheel (red or black) or tossing a dice (say a 6 or any other number i.e. 1–5) may all be tested for randomness by the Runs-test.

Again I think the method is best illustrated by an actual example. Suppose we toss a coin 50 times. The results are as follows:

1	T	0	11	T	0	21	H	1	31	H	1	41	H	1
2	T	0	12	H	1	22	T	0	32	T	0	42	H	1
3	H	1	13	H	1	23	T	0	33	H	1	43	H	1
4	H	1	14	T	0	24	H	1	34	T	0	44	T	0
5	H	1	15	H	1	25	T	0	35	T	0	45	H	1
6	H	1	16	T	0	26	T	0	36	H	1	46	H	1
7	H	1	17	H	1	27	H	1	37	T	0	47	T	0
8	H	1	18	H	1	28	H	1	38	H	1	48	T	0
9	T	0	19	T	0	29	T	0	39	H	1	49	H	1
10	H	1	20	H	1	30	H	1	40	H	1	50	T	0

Here H=heads, T=tails. Each trial is numbered 1, 2, 3 . . . 48, 49, 50. In this test for randomness one result is assigned a 1 and the other a 0. Thus in the above results a head = 1.

Running the program:

RUN
HOW MANY READINGS :
50
GIVE VALUE NO. 1
0
GIVE VALUE NO. 2
0
.
.
.
.
GIVE VALUE NO. 49
1
GIVE VALUE NO. 50
0

The computer should then print:

Z=1.04
NO. OF ITEM 1 = 30
NO. OF ITEM 2 = 20
NO. OF RUNS = 29
NO REASON TO SUPPOSE THAT RESULTS ARE NOT RANDOM

Now Z is the statistical quantity given that symbol. In this case N1= the number of heads = 30; N2 = the number of tails = 20. R = the number of runs i.e. the number of changes from 0 to 1 or from 1 to 0.

Line 260 can be eliminated if you are not using a *ZX81*. On most systems line 600 should read : 600 END.

Please note that for accuracy the Runs-test requires at least 40 data readings to be taken.

```
  1 REM RUNS TEST
200 DIM E(50)
205 PRINT "HOW MANY READINGS?"
210 INPUT W
220 LET C=-1.5
230 FOR N=1 TO W
240 PRINT "GIVE VALUE NO.";N;"
"
250 INPUT E(N)
260 CLS
270 NEXT N
300 LET N1=0
310 LET N2=0
320 LET R=1
350 FOR N=1 TO W
355 IF E(N)=1 THEN LET N1=N1+1
360 IF E(N)=0 THEN LET N2=N2+1
370 NEXT N
380 FOR N=2 TO W
385 IF E(N)=1 AND E(N-1)=0 THEN LET R=R+1
390 IF E(N)=0 AND E(N-1)=1 THEN LET R=R+1
395 NEXT N
400 LET N3=N1+N2
410 LET Q=(2*N1*N2)/N3
420 IF R<Q THEN LET C=.5
430 LET A1=((ABS (Q-R))+C)
440 LET A2=SQR (Q*(((2*N1*N2)-N3)/((N3**2)-N3)))
450 LET Z=A1/A2
470 PRINT "Z=";Z
480 PRINT "NO. OF ITEM 1=";N1
490 PRINT "NO. OF ITEM 2=";N2
495 PRINT "NO. OF RUNS=";R
500 IF Z<1.96 THEN PRINT "NO REASON TO SUPPOSE THAT RESULTS ARE NOT RANDOM."
```

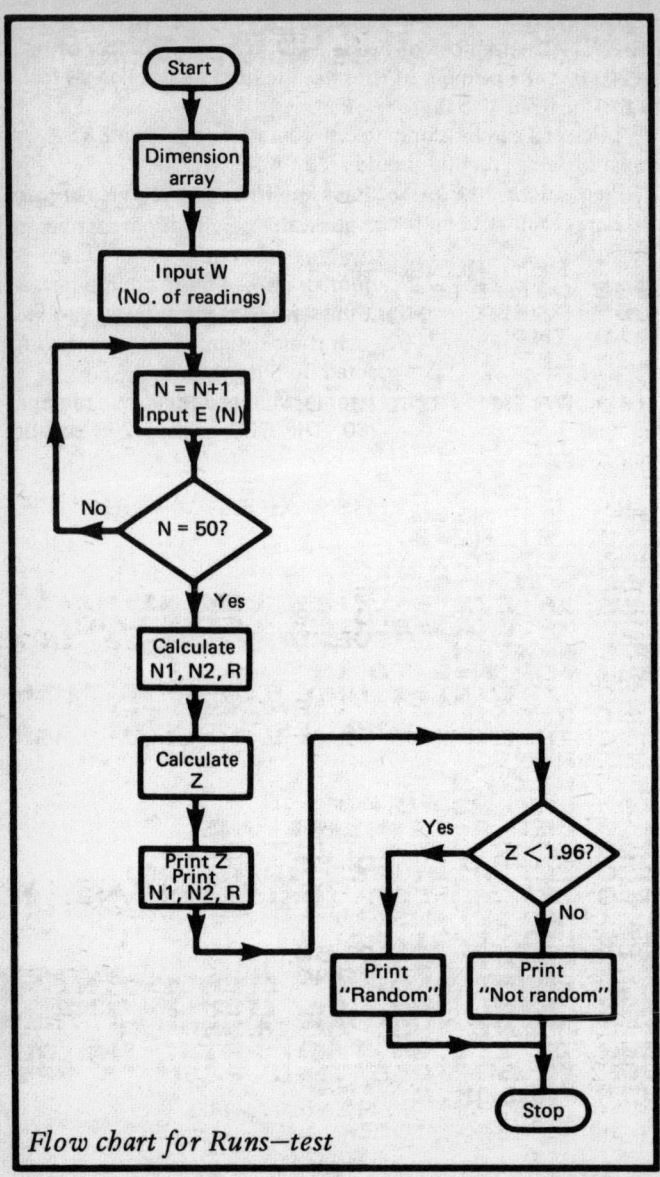

Flow chart for Runs–test

```
510 IF Z>=1.96 THEN PRINT "RESU
LTS APPEAR TO BE NON RANDOM."
600 STOP
```

ESP

This program provides an experiment in ESP (Extra Sensory Perception). In it you try to guess the next random number in the range 1—10 chosen by the computer. Your guess is checked against the actual number chosen by the computer. If you are right E(N) gets a 1 otherwise a 0. The runs test is used to check if the result of 50 such trials is significant i.e. showing a greater accuracy than expected by pure chance.

Once again non-Sinclair people will need their own random number function in line 260. The CLS on line 268 can be ignored by non-*ZX81* users.

```
200 REM ESP TEST USING RUNS TES
T
205 LET P=1
210 DIM E(50)
220 LET C=-.5
230 FOR N=1 TO 50
240 PRINT "GIVE VALUE 1-10 INCL
."
250 INPUT X
260 LET Y=INT ((RND*10)+1)
265 IF X=Y THEN LET E(N)=1
268 CLS
270 NEXT N
300 LET N1=0
310 LET N2=0
320 LET R=1
350 FOR N=1 TO 50
355 IF E(N)=1 THEN LET N1=N1+1
360 IF E(N)=0 THEN LET N2=N2+1
370 NEXT N
380 FOR N=2 TO 50
385 IF E(N)=1 AND E(N-1)=0 THEN
LET R=R+1
390 IF E(N)=0 AND E(N-1)=1 THEN
LET R=R+1
395 NEXT N
400 LET N3=N1+N2
410 LET Q=(2*N1*N2)/N3
420 IF R<Q THEN LET C=.5
```

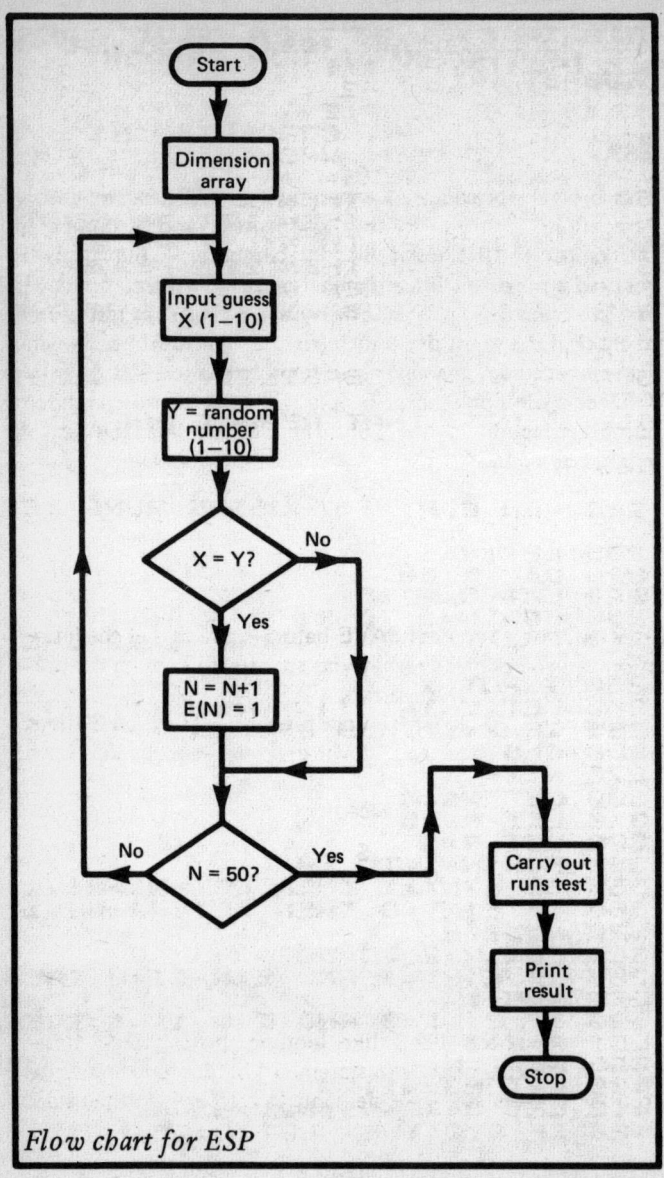

Flow chart for ESP

```
430 LET A1=((ABS (Q-R))+C)
440 LET A2=SQR (Q*(((2*N1*N2)-N3)/((N3**2)-N3)))
450 LET Z=A1/A2
470 PRINT "Z=";Z
480 PRINT "NO. CORRECT=";N1
490 PRINT "NO. WRONG=";N2
495 PRINT "RUNS=";R
500 IF Z>1.63 THEN LET P=.1
510 IF Z>1.95 THEN LET P=.05
520 IF Z>2.57 THEN LET P=.01
530 IF Z>3.08 THEN LET P=.002
535 IF P<>1 THEN GOTO 550
540 PRINT "PROBABILITY>10 PER CENT."
545 GOTO 560
550 PRINT "PROBABILITY=";P*100;"PER CENT."
560 PRINT "THAT RESULT DUE TO CHANCE."
600 STOP
```

Odds and Ends

After entering a program SAVE before running it as the latter action can sometimes prevent you successfully saving the program if it contains certain errors.

It's a good idea to SAVE your programs after each 20 lines in case the computer goes down and you lose all you have entered.

If your computer won't accept:

   85 LET G$=O$+J$+" "+L$

Try:

   85 LET G$=O$+J$
   86 LET G$=G$+" "
   87 LET G$=G$+L$

Some computers don't like looping through DIM statements. In this case place DIM statements before loop and write a routine to reset the array elements to zero or " " at the start of the loop.

Please note overleaf is a list of other titles that are available in our range of Radio, Electronics and Computer Books.

These should be available from all good Booksellers, Radio Component Dealers and Mail Order Companies.

However, should you experience difficulty in obtaining any title in your area, then please write directly to the publisher enclosing payment to cover the cost of the book plus adequate postage.

If you would like a complete catalogue of our entire range of Radio, Electronics and Computer Books then please send a Stamped Addressed Envelope to:

BERNARD BABANI (publishing) LTD
THE GRAMPIANS
SHEPHERDS BUSH ROAD
LONDON W6 7NF
ENGLAND

Code	Title	Price
205	First Book of Hi-Fi Loudspeaker Enclosures	95p
221	28 Tested Transistor Projects	1.25p
222	Solid State Short Wave Receivers for Beginners	1.25p
223	50 Projects Using IC CA3130	1.25p
224	50 CMOS IC Projects	1.35p
225	A Practical Introduction to Digital IC's	1.25p
226	How to Build Advanced Short Wave Receivers	1.95p
227	Beginners Guide to Building Electronic Projects	1.95p
228	Essential Theory for the Electronics Hobbyist	1.95p
RCC	Resistor Colour Code Disc	20p
BP1	First Book of Transistor Equivalents and Substitutes	1.50p
BP6	Engineers and Machinists Reference Tables	75p
BP7	Radio and Electronic Colour Codes and Data Chart	40p
BP14	Second Book of Transistor Equivalents and Substitutes	1.75p
BP24	52 Projects Using IC741	1.25p
BP27	Chart of Radio Electronic Semiconductor and Logic Symbols	50p
BP32	How to Build Your Own Metal and Treasure Locators	1.95p
BP33	Electronic Calculator Users Handbook	1.50p
BP34	Practical Repair and Renovation of Colour TVs	1.25p
BP36	50 Circuits Using Germanium, Silicon and Zener Diodes	1.50p
BP37	50 Projects Using Relays, SCR's and TRIACs	1.95p
BP39	50 (FET) Field Effect Transistor Projects	1.75p
BP40	Digital IC Equivalents and Pin Connections	3.50p
BP41	Linear IC Equivalents and Pin Connections	3.50p
BP42	50 Simple L.E.D. Circuits	1.50p
BP43	How to Make Walkie-Talkies	1.95p
BP44	IC555 Projects	1.95p
BP45	Projects in Opto-Electronics	1.95p
BP47	Mobile Discotheque Handbook	1.35p
BP48	Electronic Projects for Beginners	1.95p
BP49	Popular Electronic Projects	1.95p
BP50	IC LM3900 Projects	1.35p
BP51	Electronic Music and Creative Tape Recording	1.95p
BP52	Long Distance Television Reception (TV-DX) for the Enthusiast	1.95p
BP53	Practical Electronic Calculations and Formulae	2.95p
BP55	Radio Stations Guide	1.75p
BP56	Electronic Security Devices	1.95p
BP57	How to Build Your Own Solid State Oscilloscope	1.95p
BP58	50 Circuits Using 7400 Series IC's	1.75p
BP59	Second Book of CMOS IC Projects	1.50p
BP60	Practical Construction of Pre-amps, Tone Controls, Filters & Attn	1.45p
BP61	Beginners Guide to Digital Techniques	95p
BP62	Elements of Electronics — Book 1	2.25p
BP63	Elements of Electronics — Book 2	2.25p
BP64	Elements of Electronics — Book 3	2.25p
BP65	Single IC Projects	1.50p
BP66	Beginners Guide to Microprocessors and Computing	1.75p
BP67	Counter Driver and Numeral Display Projects	1.75p
BP68	Choosing and Using Your Hi-Fi	1.65p
BP69	Electronic Games	1.75p
BP70	Transistor Radio Fault-Finding Chart	50p
BP71	Electronic Household Projects	1.75p
BP72	A Microprocessor Primer	1.75p
BP73	Remote Control Projects	1.95p
BP74	Electronic Music Projects	1.75p
BP75	Electronic Test Equipment Construction	1.75p
BP76	Power Supply Projects	1.75p
BP77	Elements of Electronics — Book 4	2.95p
BP78	Practical Computer Experiments	1.75p
BP79	Radio Control for Beginners	1.75p
BP80	Popular Electronic Circuits — Book 1	1.95p
BP81	Electronic Synthesiser Projects	1.75p
BP82	Electronic Projects Using Solar-Cells	1.95p
BP83	VMOS Projects	1.95p
BP84	Digital IC Projects	1.95p
BP85	International Transistor Equivalents Guide	2.95p
BP86	An Introduction to Basic Programming Techniques	1.95p
BP87	Simple L.E.D. Circuits — Book 2	1.35p
BP88	How to Use Op-Amps	2.25p
BP89	Elements of Electronics — Book 5	2.95p
BP90	Audio Projects	1.95p
BP91	An Introduction to Radio DX-ing	1.95p
BP92	Electronics Simplified — Crystal Set Construction	1.75p
BP93	Electronic Timer Projects	1.95p
BP94	Electronic Projects for Cars and Boats	1.95p
BP95	Model Railway Projects	1.95p
BP96	C B Projects	1.95p
BP97	IC Projects for Beginners	1.95p
BP98	Popular Electronic Circuits — Book 2	2.25p
BP99	Mini-Matrix Board Projects	1.95p
BP100	An Introduction to Video	1.95p
BP101	How to Identify Unmarked IC's	65p
BP102	The 6809 Companion	1.95p
BP103	Multi-Circuit Board Projects	1.95p
BP104	Electronic Science Projects	2.25p
BP105	Aerial Projects	1.95p
BP106	Modern Op-Amp Projects	1.95p
BP107	30 Solderless Breadboard Projects — Book 1	1.95p
BP108	International Diode Equivalents Guide	2.25p
BP109	The Art of Programming the 1K ZX81	1.95p
BP110	How to Get Your Electronic Projects Working	1.95p
BP111	Elements of Electronics — Book 6	3.50p
BP112	A Z-80 Workshop Manual	2.75p
BP113	30 Solderless Breadboard Projects — Book 2	2.25p
BP114	The Art of Programming the 16K ZX81	2.50p
BP115	The Pre-Computer Book	1.95p
BP116	Electronic Toys Games and Puzzles	2.25p
BP117	Practical Electronic Building Blocks — Book 1	2.25p
BP118	Practical Electronic Building Blocks — Book 2	2.25p
BP119	The Art of Programming the ZX Spectrum	2.95p
BP120	Audio Amplifier Fault-Finding Chart	65p
BP121	How to Design and Make Your Own PCBs	2.25p
BP122	Audio Amplifier Construction	2.25p
BP123	A Practical Introduction to Microprocessors	2.25p
BP124	How to Design Electronic Projects	2.25p

Appendix 1

Solitaire Solution

From	To
2,4	4,4
3,6	3,4
1,5	3,5
4,5	2,5
1,3	1,5
1,5	3,5
6,5	4,5
5,7	5,5
5,4	5,6
3,7	5,7
5,7	5,5
5,2	5,4
7,3	5,3
4,3	6,3
7,5	7,3
7,3	5,3
2,3	4,3
3,1	3,3
3,4	3,2
5,1	3,1
3,1	3,3
5,4	3,4
3,4	3,2
3,2	5,2
5,2	5,4
5,4	5,6
4,6	4,4
4,3	4,5
3,5	5,5
5,6	5,4
6,4	4,4

Appendix 2

Alternative Version of Complex Number Routine

Alternative version of Complex number routine. Illustrates problems with ATN function (see text chapter 6). Within computer's limits can easily be amended to convert a+jb values into polar form.

```
1 REM SYMBOLIC OR J NOTATION:
10 PRINT "INPUT REAL PART OF F
IRST COMPLEX NO.:"
20 INPUT A
30 PRINT "INPUT UNREAL OR J PA
RT OF FIRST COMPLEX NO.:"
40 INPUT B
50 PRINT "INPUT REAL PART OF S
ECOND COMPLEX NO.:"
60 INPUT C
70 PRINT "INPUT UNREAL OR J PA
RT OF SECOND COMPLEX NO.:"
80 INPUT D
100 REM MENU...
110 PRINT "ENTER 1 FOR ADDITION
"
120 PRINT "2 FOR SUBTRACTION"
130 PRINT "3 FOR MULTIPLICATION
"
140 PRINT "OR 4 FOR DIVISION:"
150 INPUT V
160 IF V=1 THEN GOSUB 500
170 IF V=2 THEN GOSUB 600
180 IF V=3 THEN GOSUB 700
190 IF V=4 THEN GOSUB 700
200 IF X<0 THEN GOTO 240
210 PRINT "RESULT=";Z;"+J";X
220 GOTO 9999
240 PRINT "RESULT=";Z;"-J";ABS
(X)
300 GOTO 9999
500 REM ADD SUBR...
510 LET Z=A+C
520 LET X=B+D
590 RETURN
600 REM SUBTRACTION SUBR...
610 LET Z=A-C
```

```
620 LET X=B-D
690 RETURN
700 REM MULTIPLICATION SUBR.
710 LET Y=ATN (B/A)
720 LET M=SQR (A*A+B*B)
730 LET U=ATN (D/C)
740 LET N=SQR (C*C+D*D)
750 IF V=4 THEN GOTO 800
755 LET R=M*N
760 LET T=Y+U
790 GOTO 870
800 LET R=M/N
810 LET T=Y-U
870 LET Z=R*(COS (T))
880 LET X=R*(SIN (T))
890 RETURN
9999 STOP
```

OTHER BOOKS OF INTEREST

BP86: AN INTRODUCTION TO BASIC PROGRAMMING TECHNIQUES
S. Daly, M.B.C.S.

This book is based on the author's own experience in learning Basic and in helping others, mostly beginners, to program and understand the language.

Also included is a program library containing various programs that the author has actually written and run — these are for biorhythms, plotting a graph of y against x, standard deviation, regression, generating a musical note sequence and a card game.

The book is completed by a number of appendices which include test questions and answers on each chapter and a glossary.

96 pages   *1981*
0 85934 061 9   **£1.95**

BP109: THE ART OF PROGRAMMING THE 1K ZX81
M. James & S. M. Gee

This book shows you how to use the features of the ZX81 in programs that fit into the 1K machine and are still fun to use. In Chapter Two we explain its random number generator and use it to simulate coin tossing and dice throwing and to play pontoon. There is a great deal of fun to be had in Chapter Three, from the patterns you can display using the ZX81's graphics. Its animated graphics capabilities, explored in Chapter Four, have lots of potential for use in games of skill, such as Lunar Lander and Cannon-ball which are given as complete programs. Chapter Five explains PEEK and POKE and uses them to display large characters. The ZX81's timer is explained in Chapter Six and used for a digital clock and a reaction time game. Chapter Seven is about handling character strings and includes three more ready-to-run programs — Hangman, Coded Messages and a number guessing game. In Chapter Eight there are extra programming hints to help you get even more out of your 1K ZX81.

We hope that you'll find that this book rises to the challenge of the ZX81 and that it teaches you enough artful programming for you to be able to go on to develop programs of your very own.

96 pages   *1982*
0 85934 084 8   **£1.95**

BP114: THE ART OF PROGRAMMING THE 16K ZX81
M. James & S. M. Gee

This is a companion volume to BP109, *The Art of Programming the 1K ZX81* which introduces the possibilities that are opened up by adding the 16K RAM pack to the ZX81. The topics covered include full screen, scrolling and paged graphics and how to PEEK and POKE characters on to the screen, tape storage and number formatting — which allow you to use your ZX81 for statistics and financial programs — a further discussion on randomness, introducing the idea of simulations and an easy way of calculating π, and methods of designing and debugging a program. The use of the ZX printer is also explained in this book, including upper and lower case character sets, and the final chapter introduces machine code. Plenty of entertaining and useful programs are included.

144 pages   *1982*
0 85934 089 9   **£2.50**

BP119: THE ART OF PROGRAMMING THE ZX SPECTRUM
M. James, B.Sc., M.B.C.S.

The incredible ZX Spectrum presents its user with virtually unlimited scope. It allows versatile use of colour, offers high and low resolution graphics and also adds sound. The result can mean some very effective and exciting programs from BASIC — if you just know how!

The problem is that there is a little more than meets the eye in getting your Spectrum to do clever things. It is one thing to have learnt how to use all the Spectrum's commands but a very different one to be able to combine them into programs that do exactly what you want them to. This is just what this book is all about — teaching you the art of effective programming with your Spectrum.

The text is divided into the following chapters: 1, Getting to Know Your Spectrum; 2, Low Resolution Graphics; 3, Fun at Random; 4, High Resolution Graphics; 5, Sound; 6, Moving Graphics; 7, PEEK and POKE; 8, A Sense of Time; 9, Strings and Things; 10, Advanced Graphics.

Essential reading for all Spectrum users be they beginners or seasoned programmers.

144 pages   *1983*
0 85934 094 5   **£2.50**

BP124: EASY ADD-ON PROJECTS FOR SPECTRUM, ZX81 & ACE
O. Bishop

This book describes how to build a number of electronic projects which you can use with your Spectrum, ZX81 or Jupiter Ace microcomputer.

The projects include a Pulse Detector, Picture Digitiser, Five-key Pad, Model Controller, Bleeper, Lamp Flasher, Light Pen, Magnetic Catch, Lap Sensor, Photo-flash, Games Control and six more projects that make up a Weather Station.

All the projects are fairly simple and inexpensive to construct. The most complicated part, the Address Decoder, is constructed as a separate item that can then be used with any of the projects.

Once built, the projects are easy to operate and a simple program or two is included to get you started. Of course, those readers who are more experienced at programming can have a lot of fun in writing elaborate programs for these projects, but the beginner can start with a short program and perhaps add extra features later.

192 pages   *1983*
0 85934 099 6   **£2.75**

Notes